D. H. LAWRENCE

The Writer and his Work

by

ALASTAIR NIVEN

PUBLISHED FOR
THE BRITISH COUNCIL
BY LONGMAN GROUP LTD

LONGMAN GROUP LTD
Longman House, Burnt Mill, Harlow, Essex
Associated companies, branches and
representatives throughout the world

First published 1980
© Alastair Niven 1980

Printed in Wales by
A. McLay & Co. Ltd, Cardiff and London

ISBN 0 582 01287 2

a *Writers and their Work* Special

'I have finished my Rainbow'. This drawing, in which the rainbow spans the mining community of Eastwood and the adjoining countryside, was given in March 1915 by Lawrence to Viola Meynell, the owner of the cottage at Greatham, Sussex, where he completed the novel.   *H. T. Moore and Laurence Pollinger Ltd.*

CONTENTS

Quotations and references are from the Penguin editions of D. H. Lawrence's writings.

D. H. LAWRENCE

1. THE WRITER AND THE MAN

No one attending the birth of David Herbert (Richards) Lawrence on 11 September 1885 could have anticipated that this fourth child and third son of a miner in the Nottinghamshire town of Eastwood would become the most frequently studied English novelist of the twentieth century. As this short study of his work emphasizes he also became a proficient poet and playwright as well as one of the most prolific literary correspondents of modern times, a combative essayist and a uniquely atmospheric travel-writer. His talents extended to book-reviewing, translation, philosophical discourse, painting and teaching, but it was in the powers of his imagination and in his ability to match these with many appropriate aesthetic forms that his true genius lay. Lawrence has taken time to be recognized as a great writer, and in his own lifetime often resorted to writing short articles in order to earn some of the money which his full-length works never made. His final and subsequently most famous novel, *Lady Chatterley's Lover*, had initially to be privately published in Florence. If this was principally because of its sexual content, it nevertheless summed up the precarious relationship which Lawrence had with the publishing world. His best books were too controversial to be best sellers, the others too elusive to be categorized alongside the fiction of his times. Only in the last twenty years has his work attained the reputation which now makes it a pivot of most modern English literature courses in all kinds of educational establishments throughout the world.

Lawrence is not an easy writer to read, but he never meant to be. At a time when the socially realistic novels of John Galsworthy, Arnold Bennett and H. G. Wells were in vogue, Lawrence wanted to explore beneath the surface of human behaviour in an attempt to gauge the forces which may motivate it. In his essay entitled 'Morality and the Novel' (1925) he denounces 'the smart and smudgily cynical novel, which says it doesn't matter what you do, because one thing is as good as another, anyhow, and "prostitution" is just as much "life" as anything else.' Lawrence's work is at all times totally concerned with discriminating between levels of existence. The majority of people live half-lives, failing to develop even a tenth of the potential which they retain inwardly without knowing it. Hence the prevalence in his work of images which suggest stunted growth, seeds within husks, fruits within rinds, roots struggling below stones for light and air, but too often only withering and dying. 'A thing isn't life,' he continues in 'Morality and the Novel', 'just because somebody does it. This the artist ought to know perfectly well. The ordinary bank clerk buying himself a new straw [hat] isn't "life" at all: it is just existence, quite all right, like everyday dinners: but not "life".' This view shows how out of line Lawrence was with the age that produced *The Forsyte Saga*, *Clayhanger* and *Kipps*.

Lawrence's need to explore man's nature below its surfaces leads him into far franker discussion of sex, religion and psychology than we find in any English novelist before him. He had the advantage over most of his predecessors in having inherited a scientific terminology for these topics to draw upon when he wished, but more normally he creates his own vocabulary, the authentic Lawrentian voice which is so readily recognizable to the practised reader of his works. One may fairly doubt, however, whether Lawrence contributed to our knowledge any truly original notion about our basic human impulses. The author of 'The Woman who Rode Away' (short story, 1928), 'Democracy' (essay, date unestablished), the Loerke chapters in *Women in Love*, or *The Plumed Serpent* could verge on the bizarre, but from an empirical point of view he more frequently followed initiatives already taken by other intellectuals. This in no way detracts from his radical importance in the development of English literature, for he kept pace with the welter of ideas which transformed society in his lifetime far more effectively than any other contemporary writer and brought them directly into his work. His subsequent reputation depended a great deal upon critics and readers recognising how, especially in major

Lawrence's birthplace: The house in Victoria Street, Eastwood, where Lawrence was born in 1885. *David Wade*

Arthur Lawrence. D. H. Lawrence's father. The Walter Morel of *Sons and Lovers* 'had wavy black hair . . . and a vigorous black beard that had never been shaved.'   *Local Studies Library, Nottingham Public Library*

achievements like *The Rainbow* and *Women in Love*, he debates many sides of the major issues of the early twentieth-century. His work is highly individualized, as all great art must be; it is often eccentric and sometimes reactionary; but the person who has read his way through all of Lawrence has witnessed the transformation of English attitudes to education, morality, science and culture through the eyes of someone who accepted nothing uncritically and who retained to the end of his life a deep scepticism about the nature of the changes.

Lawrence's writing may be termed 'open-ended', even if it is not always open-minded. Though F. R. Leavis effectively linked Lawrence's moral concern with Jane Austen and George Eliot, he lacks that sense of a confident overview which permeates the work of his nineteenth-century predecessors. Austen and Eliot, in their different ways, do not doubt their own moral perspective. Lawrence, while superficially appearing to be a more dogmatic and authoritarian writer, constantly extends himself to the limits of his understanding, seeming at times to contradict himself. In *Women in Love*, for example, he paints a powerfully seductive portrait of a society harnessed to science in order to serve man's greed, though his intention is to deplore the mechanical life to which it gives birth; at the end of *The Plumed Serpent* he appears to renounce the thesis upon which the novel has been built; he wrote *Lady Chatterley's Lover* three times because his focal point kept shifting. Indeed, in the sexual descriptions of this last novel, as in the pastoral rhapsodies of his first, *The White Peacock*, or in the mystical ceremonies of *The Plumed Serpent*, the resources of language themselves nearly crack under the strain of expressing feelings which are wholly non-verbal in experience. Neither Austen nor Eliot – indeed, no English novelist before Lawrence, with the possible exception of Emily Brontë – had risked such a stretching of language. Lawrence brings to modern prose an instinct to express the nearly inexpressible which previously only some poets had tried. If his work sometimes threatens to collapse into a heap of rhetorical, repetitive and inflated utterance, it is more because even the prodigiously flexible English language cannot cope with the moments he is seeking to render than because his art has failed.

Many elements in Lawrence's life-story found their way into his writing, for he hardly ever wrote about things he had not witnessed or about situations which did not ultimately derive from personal experience. We know him, however, as a novelist, poet, playwright or essayist, not as an autobiographer. He would plant allusions to his own life in his books – the Beardsall family in *The White Peacock*, for example, take their name from his mother, Lydia Beardsall, who herself became the basis for Mrs. Morel in *Sons and Lovers* and partly for Lydia Lensky in *The Rainbow*. However, he never allowed his imagination to be dominated by documentary accuracy. Specific details about Lawrence's life can only be found in his writing when he thought them useful to mention, and one wonders, therefore, if their relevance has not been overstressed by many critics.

D. H. Lawrence was brought up in respectable hardship. The atmosphere of Eastwood in the late nineteenth-century is best described in his essay 'Nottingham and the Mining Country' (1929), where he rues the social and aesthetic disaster by which old England was made ugly and dehumanized by the spread of industrialism. The theme of erosion obsesses Lawrence all through his writing career, erosion of nature, erosion of humanity.

Now though perhaps nobody knew it, it was ugliness which betrayed the spirit of man in the nineteenth century. The great crime which the moneyed classes and promoters of industry committed in the palmy Victorian days was the condemning of the workers to ugliness, ugliness, ugliness: meanness and formless and ugly surroundings, ugly ideals, ugly religion, ugly hope, ugly love, ugly clothes, ugly furniture, ugly houses, ugly relationships between workers and employers. The human soul needs actual beauty even more than bread.

Lawrence recognized, moreover, that beauty means different things to different people, and that for this reason his parents' marriage had already drifted into a state of implacable resentment when he, the fourth son, was born in 1885. Mrs. Lawrence came originally from a lower middle-

Moorgreen Colliery. The model for Minton's Colliery, the workplace of
Walter Morel in *Sons and Lovers*. Lawrence's father worked in the nearby
Brinsley Colliery. *Nottingham University Library*

Miners sharing out wages. 'All the earnings of each stall were put down to
the chief butty, as contractor, and he divided the wages . . . ' (*Sons and
Lovers, ch. 4*) *National Coal Board*

The Lawrence family. A studio portrait of the family, taken in the 1890's, showing: standing, Emily Una, George (the eldest son), William Ernest (seven years older than D. H. Lawrence); and seated, Lettice Ada (the youngest child), Mrs Lydia Lawrence, D. H. Lawrence, Mr Arthur Lawrence.

class family in Kent. She had trained as a schoolteacher and continued until her death in 1910 to venerate study and art. Her husband had little formal education and viewed with suspicion anything that was not fundamentally necessary to the practicalities of living. Such a summary, however, has immediately to be qualified, lest it suggest that Lawrence's father was a puritan fundamentalist and his mother an intellectual dabbler. Almost the opposite was true. Lawrence's father had an instinct for comradeship with his workmates which became stronger as he felt more excluded from the life which Mrs. Lawrence created for herself and her children. He knew little more than the Bible, some hymns and a few robust ballads, whereas she admired all expressions of learning, but she did so with a seriousness more profoundly puritanical than was evident in his love of plain living and easy friendship. Mrs. Lawrence venerated the Protestant ethic of hard work and Nonconformist morality. Pleasure that was not directed towards self-improvement verged on sin. In her son's novels we find this conflict between two almost opposed views of life expressed many times; though it is most obvious in *Sons and Lovers*, it is the issue upon which Rupert Birkin clashes with Gerald Crich in *Women in Love* and it underlies every crisis in Lawrence's work where reason and will, intellect and passion are at odds. The source of these differences was partly social, or so Lawrence rationalized it at the end of his life in 'Nottingham and the Mining Country', where he talks of the 'curious close intimacy' between men in a working community and of the instinct for 'possession and egoism' in the women left at home. Men disappear in their working lives into the dark womb of the earth, while the women remain on its surface crust, looking outwards and beyond, straining for what might be rather than content with what actually is: it is as though our daily existences in an industrial community embody the gulf that has opened up between male and female.

Lawrence's mother idolized her elder son Ernest, who died in 1901. She cared about the education of all her children, however. Lawrence himself attended a local Board School, and them from 1898 to 1901 was a scholar at

Nottingham High School. After a brief period as a clerk in a Nottingham factory he became a student-teacher in Eastwood, and from 1906 to 1908 he studied at Nottingham University College. It was in these years that he befriended Jessie Chambers, whom he uncharitably represented as the spiritual Miriam in *Sons and Lovers*. The Chambers family lived on a farm called The Haggs, where Lawrence spent many of his spare moments. For the first time he experienced an environment where love of nature and discussion of serious issues need not be indulged defensively. He also came under the influence of William Hopkin, a local bootshop manager who introduced him to the principles of Socialism and invited him to attend meetings where he met several Labour leaders. Lawrence always followed political life closely and became increasingly interested in the possibilities of political action in his later novels, but he remained dissatisfied with the values of the British political parties all his life, finding them hierarchical and simplistic.

Jessie Chambers, Alice Dax, Louie Burrows, Hopkin's wife Sallie, Lawrence's sister Ada – in the years of his young manhood Lawrence was not short of female company. Mrs. Dax is believed to have initiated him sexually and to Louie Burrows he was briefly and rather unconvincingly engaged. Jessie probably exerted the greatest influence on him because she took the greatest interest in his early attempts at writing, reading his first poems, the earliest draft of his play *A Collier's Friday Night* and the manuscript of *The White Peacock*. In 1908 Lawrence moved to Croydon, just south of London, where for the next four years he taught art, English and biology at Davidson Road School. He made new friendships – mainly with women – and began tentatively to make contact with the literary world in London, He met Ford Madox Hueffer, editor of *The English Review*. Ezra Pound, Edward Garnett; he corresponded with many other writers, gave lectures about some of them, and continually enlarged his reading.

Lawrence's first published work consisted of poems and reviews in *The English Review*. *The White Peacock*, his first novel, was published in January 1911. *The Trespasser*, his second, in May 1912, and *Sons and Lovers*, his personal

Lawrence in 1906. In his own words 'a clean-shaven, bright young prig in a high collar like a curate'. *Nottingham University Library*

Frieda Weekley (born von Richthofen) in 1912. *Keith Sagar*

masterpiece in many people's judgement, in May 1913. This rapid production belies the difficulty with which Lawrence perfected his work to his own satisfaction. Each novel and most of his stories and poems went through several drafts. He was, however, a compulsive writer and had been so since the age of nineteen when he wrote his first poems. For some writers such a prolific output might betoken an inability to relate to the social world, but this was never really true of Lawrence. His friendships were sometimes shortlived and quarrelsome but even in the years when he lived in remote places he enjoyed the fellowship of good company. No major English writer has left so voluminous a correspondence or, in modern times at least, had the minutiae of his daily life so frequently observed in the memoirs of the people he met. Though Lawrence left Davidson Road School in 1912 and never again had that kind of regular employment, it would be quite wrong to suppose that he opted out of vigorous social intercourse.

In March 1912 Lawrence met Frieda Weekley, the wife of a Nottingham professor. Only two months later they left England together to visit Germany, where Lawrence was briefly arrested as a spy. Frieda came from a family of minor German nobility called von Richthofen. She was the mother of three children, whom she 'abandoned' by going away with Lawrence, but with whom she remained in close contact all her life. It was in every sense an unconventional liaison which shocked contemporary morality, for it not only disrupted the Weekley marriage but it cut across class. When Lawrence and Frieda eventually married in July 1914 they compounded their social unacceptability by going against the current of Anglo-German hostility. The relationship could hardly have been more ill-starred from society's point of view, and it was undoubtedly a major factor in the Lawrences' eventual decision to leave England and live abroad.

By 1914 D. H. Lawrence was an established author, singled out by the elderly Henry James as one of the most promising novelists in England, the friend of many leading intellectuals and the favoured house guest of fashionable patrons. He was at work on his grandest conception, provisionally entitled

The Sisters but later to be divided into two quite different works, *The Rainbow* and *Women in Love*. He was flattered by this life and invigorated by his own intellectual capacities. He was, however, wary of being taken over by the Bloomsbury crowd, whom he found conceited and soft-centred. He contemplated founding an experimental school with Bertrand Russell, but soon realized how emotionally apart they were from each other, so that the friendship collapsed into cold abuse. He seemed to Russell 'a sensitive would-be despot who got angry with the world because it would not instantly obey' (Russell's *Autobiography*, Vol. II, Chapter 1). Though Russell's case against Lawrence seems, in the light of Lawrence's complex writings, greatly overstated – 'he had no real wish to make the world better, but only to indulge in eloquent soliloquy about how bad it was' – it is only fair to say that many of their contemporaries viewed him in a similar way.

The Lawrences had a peripatetic war, though regulations prevented them from leaving England. As we shall see in the discussion of his novel *Kangaroo*, Lawrence had the most profound horror at the way the war was conducted. It seemed to him an explosion of all the obscene, violent, destructive and materialistic characteristics of western machine-worshipping society, while at the same time he was equally outraged by the loss of young life. He offered himself for war service and was rejected on medical grounds. Instead he and Frieda stayed in London, then in a borrowed house near Padstow and finally near St. Ives. These were years of conflict with society. When *The Rainbow* was published in 1915 it was abused by the critics and eventually banned as a danger to public morality.

At the end of the war Lawrence at once made plans to leave England, though it was November 1919 before he and Frieda left for Italy. Here, in various places including Florence, Capri and Sicily, and with a period of three months in Germany, the Lawrences stayed until February 1922. By the standards of his earlier years this period was not so productive. Lawrence had completed *Women in Love* before he went abroad (it was published in New York in 1920). In Italy he completed *The Lost Girl* and revised his

Studies in Classic American Literature, wrote *Aaron's Rod*, drawing on his observations in Florence, composed the poems which became *Birds, Beasts and Flowers*, and produced some of his best short fiction including 'Fanny and Annie', 'The Captain's Doll', and 'The Fox'. None of these works, however, are written on the scale of *Sons and Lovers*, *The Rainbow* and *Women in Love*. Though there are few signs in this period of Lawrence's imaginative fertility drying up, he was undoubtedly feeling deeply unsettled. At the root of this apprehension was his profound conviction that the war had solved nothing and merely confirmed the wrong course which modern society was taking. He therefore looked around for other societies where alternative options might still be open, or where, perhaps, the people might be confident enough in their own created values not to want to emulate northern Europe and America. Sicily came close to such a society, but the influence of the Church was too restricting. Lawrence therefore set sail for Australia, the newest attempt by western man to start afresh in virginal surroundings: or so he supposed it to be, until living there for a few weeks in a house facetiously called 'Wyewurk'.

From Australia the Lawrences sailed, via New Zealand and Tahiti, to San Francisco and thence they travelled to Taos in New Mexico. Here a rapacious American *padrona* called Mabel Sterne lived in a state of self-conscious 'protection' of the local Indians. Lawrence increasingly resented any form of patronage, but among the descendants of the Aztecs in New Mexico and in Mexico itself he probably came closest to his ideal of discovering a way of life which was still in communion with its own ancestry; this was because the Mexico of the mid-1920's was undergoing a nationalist revival in which it was seriously suggested that the ancient religion of Quetzalcoatl might be a viable alternative to fascism or to vehement pro-American influences. Lawrence rejoiced in the ruins of the former civilization he saw in Mexico and seriously explored the mystical aspects of the old religion. Out of these experiences came two of his most obscure and symbolic works of fiction, *The Plumed Serpent* (1926) and 'The Woman who Rode Away', but in the end he realized the impossibility of grafting an alien culture on to instincts which had taken centuries to germinate in his own part of the world. He found himself, in other words, as much in touch with the civilization he thought he had rejected, and whose material expressions he would continue to deplore, as the Mexican Indians were in touch with their Serpent God.

In 1924 Lawrence made a brief return to Europe and he finally left Mexico in September 1925, six months after tuberculosis was positively diagnosed as the origin of his continuing physical debilitation. Lawrence had never enjoyed good health and in his search for other modes of living he always went to warm climates where his condition improved. From 1925 onwards, however, his illness prevailed. It affected his creativity. In the last five years of his life he wrote only one novel, *Lady Chatterley's Lover* – though admittedly there are three versions of the book. He wrote some of his best essays, including 'Pornography and Obscenity', 'A Propos of *Lady Chatterley's Lover*' and 'Nottingham and the Mining Country'. Poems and stories, the latter including 'The Escaped Cock' and 'Rawdon's Roof', his philosophical commentary *Apocalypse*, and many of his best poems date from these last years. He continued to review books, to write letters, to translate from the Italian and to see friends. He lived from late 1925 to mid-1928 mainly in Italy and thereafter principally in France where, at Vence on 2 March 1930, he died aged forty-four.

In the last months of his life D. H. Lawrence was visited by H. G. Wells, Norman Douglas, Aldous Huxley, Mulk Raj Anand, Mark Gertler, the Aga Khan and many others. He was very famous but still almost totally unaccepted by the general reader. It took three decades before Lawrence's work automatically appeared on educational syllabi. He remains a controversial figure, not least to the modern feminist movement, which has usually taken issue with him. In 1960 he was the subject of the most publicized literary prosecution in the English courts when Penguin Books successfully defended their unexpurgated edition of *Lady Chatterley's Lover*. Lawrence is now, however, almost certainly the most widely taught twentieth-century writer that England has produced. All his books are in print. A definitive edition of his works is being published by the Cambridge University Press. He will be the subject of a major television series. Film versions have been made of *Sons and Lovers, Women in Love,* 'The Fox' and 'The Virgin and the Gypsy'. An academic journal is devoted to his work. At every point on whatever scale we measure popularity and greatness Lawrence's name appears. Fifty years on from his death he more and more appears as one of the major figures in the history of literature. This short account of his work attempts to show why this may be so, and why the questioning and dispute which his name continues to arouse helps to justify rather than to undermine his reputation.

2. *THE WHITE PEACOCK*

Lawrence's first novel is his only one to be told in the first person. *The White Peacock* came out in 1911, a few months after the death of Lawrence's mother, who was nevertheless able to read an advance copy. The new young author revised his work several times before submitting it to the publisher William Heinemann, and something of this over-refinement can be detected in the more flamboyantly lyrical passages of the novel. Lawrence always liked to reconsider what he had written once the first draft of a novel was complete, but this was usually because he was battling to find an appropriate form to express complex ideas and had even, on occasions, radically changed his views about what he wanted to say. In *The White Peacock* his revisions tend less to the recasting of thought than to a self-conscious decoration of the prose. This is a novel full of adolescent rhapsodizing about love and nature, but it contains many precursors of the mature Lawrence. Its excesses are characteristic of an ambitious writer finding his feet and of someone wanting to harness his exultation in language to his curiosity about human behaviour.

Before Lawrence the opportunities for working-class writers to write about working-class life and then to see their work in print were extremely rare. Lawrence therefore made middle-class people the subject of his first novel; in his next book, *The Trespasser*, the social level is less privileged, but the values against which the protagonists react are still essentially middle-class; only in *Sons and Lovers* did he find an authentic voice for working-class aspirations. The three central characters in *The White Peacock* – Lettie Beardsall, George Saxton and Leslie Tempest – are described to us by Lettie's brother Cyril. Lawrence handicaps himself by using an 'I' narrator, for after Lettie marries Leslie it becomes difficult to sustain the intimate observation of their relationship, which Cyril's presence beforehand permits. The novel thus loses much of its impetus in its last chapters. Enough has been established by then, however, for us to recognize the error of Lettie's decision to reject the more sensual George. In doing this she denies fundamental needs within herself in order to do what is socially proper and what will bring the surface rewards of position and wealth. This conflict between self-fulfilment and social gratification reflects the more impersonal battleground of society's encroachment upon nature. In *The White Peacock* Lawrence celebrates the beauties of his native countryside with the extravagant enthusiasm of one who fears it may be threatened with destruction by creeping industrialization, a theme he summarizes symbolically by having the arch-enemy of materialism, the gamekeeper Annable, crushed by a fall of stones in a quarry.

The opening lines of Lawrence's first novel show his characteristic facility in relating the natural world to the human.

I stood watching the shadowy fish slide through the gloom of the mill-pond. They were grey, descendants of the silvery things that had darted away from the monks, in the young days when the valley was lusty. The whole place was gathered in the musing of old age. The thick-piled trees on the far shore were too dark and sober to dally with the sun; the weeds stood crowded and motionless. Not even a little wind flickered the willows of the islets. The water lay softly, intensely still. Only the thin stream falling through the millrace murmured to itself of the tumult of life which had once quickened the valley. (p 13)

At the start of *The Rainbow* and *Lady Chatterley's Lover*, and at some point in all his novels, Lawrence links the contemporary world with the natural and social history out of which it has evolved. Here at the opening of *The White Peacock* he presents an idyllic scene of unperturbed nature, 'gathered in the musing of old age'. This is a world where man has come and gone, once tilled by monks but to which man now returns only as an onlooker – or a violator. The natural world throughout this novel has a harmony and self-sufficiency which contrasts with the disruptions of the social world.

It is not impossible for man to share in this harmony. The harvest episodes or the scene with George and the narrator bathing in the pond show man and nature in almost rhythmic correspondence. 'When I began to swim', Cyril records, 'soon the water was buoyant, and I was sensible of nothing but the vigorous poetry of action' (p. 256). This sense of man finding complete freedom in a partnership with nature, as the body is supported here by the upthrust of the water, attracts Lawrence throughout his life. His works may largely be read as an exploration of how such a right balance may be found. The passage continues 'I saw George swimming on his back laughing at me, and in an instant I had flung myself like an impulse after him'. Through partnership between human beings something of this absorption within nature may be discovered: certainly an ill-balanced relationship (an unhappy marriage, a dominating lover, a possessive parent) will be no way to achieve it. In *The White Peacock* Cyril's obvious attraction towards the manly George has homosexual undertones which no doubt expressed part of Lawrence's own nature, but they are not the essential point of it.

In novel after novel Lawrence seeks for the establishment of right partnership that will accord with nature. The sexual element is only part of this. Significantly in this passage the narrator speaks of flinging himself after George 'like an impulse': not 'on an impulse', but as though he has actually *become* a force of nature. For one instant true harmony between men and their natural environment has been created: 'our love was perfect for a moment, more perfect than any love known since, either for man or woman' (p. 257). If only this moment could become a

25

continuing reality! That is Lawrence's central urge, to find permanence for those isolated moments of perfect inter-fusion which we experience perhaps only a few times in our lives, but which, as a consequence, we know could be the character of our existences. In *Lady Chatterley's Lover*, at the end of his career, the insistence on trying to describe the pleasure of orgasm is a further attempt to express this deep conviction in Lawrence, at all stages of his career, that a higher kind of experience is waiting for us if we can only find a means of achieving it.

The only certainty is that all the roads upon which society is travelling are taking it away from the realization of this perfect harmony of men with nature and with each other. Annable, the keeper in *The White Peacock* who looks forward to Mellors in *Lady Chatterley's Lover*, believes that all civilization is 'the painted fungus of rottenness' (p. 172). He has been humiliated by marriage to a pre-Raphaelite lady – an early indication of Lawrence's antipathy to the destructiveness of the gentility – and he has tried to drop out of society by living a 'natural' life in the woods. Appeal-ing to Cyril though Annable is, not least for his physical endowments, we are not invited to admire his existence as ideal. This Jaques in Arden has too cynical a view of man's failures: 'he scorned religion and all mysticism' (p. 173). Though Lawrence has not yet developed a vocabulary for talking at length about them, he felt deeply that there were mysteries within nature ready for man's discovery. If the novel often retreats into poetic excess – 'Here was spring sitting just awake, unloosening her glittering hair and opening her purple eye' (p. 180) – this is mainly because Lawrence strives too anxiously to find a lyrical tone for his quasi-religious motif. In *The Rainbow* he writes more confidently, not because he has greatly developed his sense of man's potential interaction with nature, but because his expression of it has its own personality. It no longer seems enslaved by a Pater-like concept of 'beautiful prose'. Yet many passages in *The White Peacock* also record Lawrence's wonderful eye for natural detail. Not since Hardy – who stopped writing novels in 1894 – had an English novelist written so observantly of country life.

The White Peacock sets a vivid life of social interaction and of family relationships against its eulogy of the natural world. Several episodes indicate the viciousness in man's nature – George flippantly destroying a bee, or the rabbit hunt, for example – but at the core of each main character a crucial weakness exists like a rot: George's narcissism; Leslie's sexual inadequacy (hinted at: the novel of 1911 is still governed by Victorian restraints), for which he compensates by material display; Lettie's lack of courage to be herself, Cyril's detachment; Annable's bitterness. Lawrence's first novel is a study of failure. So, too, is *The Trespasser*, but in this next novel he at least shows elements of triumph in that the main character refuses to compromise with mediocrity. *The White Peacock* shows a natural world vanishing fast and the possibility of private worlds which might have been, but it does not offer the achievement of any world worth having. Lawrence could sow the seeds of his distinction as a novelist in this kind of young man's pessimism, but he could not bring it to fruition.

3. THE TRESPASSER

The Trespasser (1912) is the shortest of Lawrence's full-length novels. It is also one of his least known. Lawrence moves away from the familiar world of the English Midlands to London and the Isle of Wight, the first of which he knew only because he had taught in a Croydon school just south of London between 1908 and 1912. In 1909 he went on a short summer holiday to the Isle of Wight and from that visit he no doubt gained some of the local colour in *The Trespasser*, but many of the circumstances of the novel were derived from a brief love affair between one of his Croydon colleagues, Helen Corke, and a music teacher. Helen Corke kept a journal of her relationship with Herbert Macartney during a week they spent together on the Isle of Wight, and it was upon this and her own conversations that Lawrence based the relationship between Siegmund McNair and Helena Verden in *The Trespasser*. Helen Corke re-created her friendship with Macartney in her own novel *Neutral*

Helen Corke. One of Lawrence's fellow teachers at Davidson Road School, Croydon. Her love affair with a music teacher inspired the plot of *The Trespasser*. *Humanities Research Center, University of Texas at Austin.*

Ground (1931), and said more about it in her autobiography, *In Our Infancy* (1975). In both works her version significantly differs from Lawrence's. As with *Sons and Lovers*, however, critics have expended much energy on the biographical elements in the book, without always appreciating that Lawrence was writing a work of imagined experience. Its source lay in fact, but the concerns of the novel show a natural development from *The White Peacock;* Lawrence would no doubt have found some other framework to explore the same issues had he not encountered Helen Corke's account of her bizarre romance.

Whereas *The White Peacock* shows a settled world being disrupted by emotional tensions and by the creeping malaise of modern life, *The Trespasser* begins in a dull suburban villa in London. Lawrence sets a substantial part of only one other novel, *Aaron's Rod*, in the capital city, and in both books the main character escapes from it as soon as possible. As Lawrence says at the end of his essay 'Dull London' (1928), 'the sense of abject futility in it all only deepens the sense of abject dullness, so all there is to do is to go away.' Helena's room, where *The Trespasser* begins, has walls 'of the dead-green colour of August foliage' and a carpet which lies 'like a square of grass in a setting of black loam' (p. 5). These comparisons with nature only highlight the drabness of the room. Siegmund's home is no different, loveless and lightless when we first read of it. Helena and Siegmund escape from their dreary world of mechanical routine to a brief idyll on the Isle of Wight, but they return to London, she in eventual denial of their love, he to his hollow marriage.

Siegmund is the only one of Lawrence's major protagonists to take his own life. He cannot endure a life without Helena, yet to abandon his wife and children is equally inconceivable.

He was bound by an agreement which there was no discrediting to provide for them. And then what? Humiliation at home, Helena forsaken, musical comedy night after night. That was insufferable – impossible! Like a man tangled up in a rope, he was not strong enough to free himself. (p 185)

Siegmund therefore hangs himself. His death requires some courage, but the fact that Lawrence never again used such an ending underlines his dissatisfaction with this solution to the novel, and maybe accounts for the relatively low estimation of it which most critics have had. In a novelist so passionately interested in seeing how a fulfilled life may be attained, the extinction of life represents a defeat not only for his main character but for his own conception of fiction. Later heroes like Paul Morel in *Sons and Lovers* and Birkin in *Women in Love* overcome their tendency to despair and reach towards a positive view of life, however difficult this may be to sustain.

The Trespasser is not an anti-feminist novel – Siegmund's wife, for example, is portrayed with some pity – but it does suggest that between male and female there too often exists an imbalance in the relationship which debilitates both partners. As Siegmund's acquaintance Hampson puts it, ' "She can't live without us, but she destroys us." ' (p. 84). This is not Lawrence's view of what has to happen when men and women conjoin, but his notion of what frequently does happen because the right balance has not been struck, give and take has not been proffered. An assertion of wills must lead to one partner's victory over the other. Since the man normally works closer to the land than the woman, whose role has traditionally been domestic, he is more in tune with the natural forces with which humanity has so often lost touch. In later novels he shows women breaking out of their expected role and thus showing a capacity to achieve with men the two-way sharing, in harmony with the natural world, that they too frequently resist – Ursula Brangwen in *The Rainbow* is the prime example. Helena in *The Trespasser* goes some way in Ursula's direction, but fatally lacks the final intensity of vision which is needed. Hampson has a point, Lawrence intends us to realize, when he goes on to say, ' "These deep, interesting women don't want *us*; they want the flowers of the spirit they can gather of us. We, as natural men, are more or less degrading to them and to their love of us; therefore they destroy the natural man in us – that is, us altogether." '

The Trespasser shares with *The White Peacock* a vivid realization of the natural world, though Lawrence less surely indulges in poetic effect for its own sake. Indeed, it tends to be in his analysis of human behaviour that Lawrence's imagery over-reaches itself. Self-conscious phrasing – 'She was the earth in which his strange flowers grew' (p. 36) or 'She felt herself confronting God at home in His white incandescence' (p. 114) – shows how artificial Lawrence could still be. The novel is full of a slightly adolescent religiosity: Siegmund, for example, deriving comfort 'from the knowledge that life was treating him in the same manner as it had treated the Master, though his compared small and despicable with the Christ-tragedy' (p. 79). At times the urgency of Lawrence's desire to express his sense of there being a mystic reality which makes human ambitions paltry leads him to be nearly incomprehensible:

... it only happens we see the iridescence on the wings of a bee. It exists whether or not, bee or no bee. Since the iridescence and the humming of life *are* always, and since it was they who made me, then I am not lost. At least, I do not care. If the spark goes out, the essence of the fire is there in the darkness. What does it matter? Besides, I *have* burned bright; I have laid up a fine cell of honey somewhere – I wonder where? (p. 144)

Rationally this passage does not make clear sense: how can 'iridescence on the wings of a bee' exist 'bee or no bee'? However, it is necessary to accept, because we encounter many such prose-moments in later works, that Lawrence is struggling to express a concept which lies beyond the normal restrictions of language – to convey that there is something deeply interfused in the universe which will continue to exist even if mankind should die out, and which certainly continues when each individual man dies. This creative force can be glimpsed at least representatively in nature – the bee's wings – but man normally makes no attempt to understand what it is or how it may be experienced fully. In *Women in Love* Birkin will reflect on what the world would be like if the human race should cease to exist: 'a world empty of people, just uninterrupted grass, and a hare sitting up' (p. 142), an image of a nature still flowing (a favourite Lawrentian word) even if man has failed to live up to it. In *The Trespasser* the novelist reaches for a way of expressing his sense of this other life, besides which human life looks ephemeral and irrelevant. It is worth noting, however, that he has not yet sorted out his scale of values. Siegmund feels increasingly 'like a slow bullet winging into the heart of life' (p. 148), as though his human existence has no meaning in the 'gorgeous and uncouth' natural world. Later novels are life-affirming, with Lawrence seeking to accommodate humanity, not to reject it. *The Trespasser* may have been for him a therapeutic novel, for within it he seems to exorcise the debilitating melancholia and nihilism of the young romantic idealist in order to move, in his next novel, to a more robust and emotionally complex contemplation of the world. Eventually, in *The Rainbow* and *Women in Love*, he will come as close as he could to defining the right balance that ought to exist between man's sense of his own worth and his understanding of the life forces which he so often fails to perceive because of his self-obsession.

The Trespasser is full of themes which Lawrence will develop more expressively in maturer novels. In itself it is too patchy to be a complete success, though the opening and closing chapters have a severity which show Lawrence's eagerness not to use language only for poetic effects. The book is another study in stunted growth. In his next novel, *Sons and Lovers*, he developed beyond this because, for the first time, he imagined his own instincts at the centre rather than at the periphery of the experiences he was describing.

4. SONS AND LOVERS

Sons and Lovers is possibly the most widely read serious English novel of the twentieth-century. In some respects it renders commentary of any kind absurd. Who, for example, can read the description of Mrs. Morel's death without being reminded of a grief they themselves have experienced? The novel obviously draws on personal recollections so deeply that it seems impertinent to analyze it. Yet our admiration for it results partly from its imaginative intensity and from its masterly control of feeling. Lawrence's narrative never becomes self-indulgent; even in the moments when he tries to be visionary or mystic the

Sons Lovers

Paul Morel

Chapter I.
Antecedents.

"The Breach" took the place of Hell Row It
was a natural succession. Hell Row was a block
of some half dozen thatched, ~~subsiding~~ cottages
which stood back in the brook-course by Greenhill
Lane. Eastwood had scarcely gathered consciousness
when the notorious ~~that~~ Row was burned down. The
village, was strewed rather forlornly over hills and
the valley, ~~sparse, meagre, and disintegrated~~. Since
the seventeenth century the people of Eastwood have
scratched at the earth for coal. The old cottage rows
along Green-hill Lane were built to accommodate
the workers in the small little gin-pits which were
scattered about among the ~~fields~~, beside Derby Road,
and Nottingham Road, and Mansfield Road. To these
vanished pits the pasture land in many parts owes
its queer configuration. But fifty years ago the
pits were busy, and in the four square miles round
Eastwood there ~~were~~ perhaps some two or three hundred
of these miners' cottages, old and mean, dabbed down

Page 1 of 'Paul Morel'. The first page of the manuscript of the early
version of *Sons and Lovers* bearing the original title. *Laurence Pollinger
Ltd and the Humanities Research Center, University of Texas at Austin.*

prose becomes only slightly overcoloured. Personally felt though *Sons and Lovers* is, Lawrence in some ways makes of it his most orthodox novel. It capitalizes on the *bildungs-roman*, a form of fiction which allows the novelist to recreate through the maturing of his protagonist some of his own remembered intensity of experience. *Sons and Lovers* marks a great advance for Lawrence on the two novels he had written before it, but in terms of the evolution of the English novel its main innovations are less a matter of fictional technique than of topic. It is one of the first wholly authentic novels of English working-class life, set mainly in an industrialized as opposed to an agricultural community and written by someone who had grown up within the society he is depicting. It marks Lawrence's arrival as a great novelist, but it may also mark the end of his ability to speak so straightforwardly of working life, for its success provided him with an *entrée* into other kinds of society to which he had already started to gravitate from the time he began teaching in Croydon.

'*Paul Morel* [as he initially planned to call *Sons and Lovers*] will be a novel – not a florid prose poem, or a decorated idyll running to seed in idealism: but a restrained, somewhat impersonal novel.' This comment, in a letter dated 18 October 1910, shows how self-critical Lawrence could be, for he plans now to write a work wholly different from *The White Peacock* or *The Trespasser*, both of which, we must conclude from the phrasing, dissatisfied him on account of their exaggerated language. *Sons and Lovers*, one must emphasize, is not an autobiography. If it were then there would be no place in it for an incident such as that where Mrs. Morel names her baby son – 'She thrust the infant forward to the crimson, throbbing sun, almost with relief' (p.51). It may be distantly related to an actual happening about which Lawrence's mother talked, but it is realized poetically and symbolically, an initiation rite, a baptism by fire, an exorcism of guilt. It goes far beyond a mere statement of personal history. This is so with every part of the novel.

In the conflict that develops early on in *Sons and Lovers* between Mr. and Mrs. Morel we see dramatized, in an

Hagg's Farm: The home of the Chambers family, who were among Lawrence's closest friends in his adolescence. The house is described as Willey Farm in *Sons and Lovers*. *Photograph Keith Sagar*

almost emblematic way, two strains in the English national character. This in no way minimizes the powerful clash of temperaments and wills that makes their marriage so tragic and, in the last chapters of the book, so pathetic. It shows *Sons and Lovers* to be not only a novel of private emotions but a study in late nineteenth-century social life. Mr. Morel displays qualities of unintellectual male-orientated sociability which contrasts with his wife's strict nonconformist morality, high intentions for her children and possessiveness. Lawrence, in his later books, came to admire the type of man which he believed his father to have been far more than would appear from his portrait of Walter Morel, who is presented initially as unreasonably ill-tempered, then as weak-willed, and finally as an empty husk from whom the kernel of life has been removed. In *Sons and Lovers* the personality of Mrs. Morel dominates all the early chapters and the end of the novel. Lawrence's account of her as

Lydia Lawrence. D. H. Lawrence's mother. A photograph taken in old age.

Note: We are grateful to the Castle Gallery Nottingham for their assistance in obtaining the photographs of the Lawrence family, Mrs Lawrence and Jessie Chambers.

magnificently strong-minded, loving but stifling, is one of the chief glories of the book, though his portrait is critical. She sums up much of the imprisoning morality and vaulting intellectual ambition which he increasingly believed to be instilled in the women of industrialized communities.

Paul Morel's growing-up and his awakening to the possibilities of the world is the main subject of *Sons and Lovers*. To convey this, Lawrence achieves a synthesis of social realism and metaphor that may be unparalleled in English fiction. There are many instances to exemplify this – Mrs. Morel's expulsion from her house on the night she becomes aware of Paul's conception is one example, Clara's initiation of Paul is another. We find it at all stages of Paul's relationship with Miriam. Here they are, at springtime, symbolically representing youth and promise, whilst at the same time tangibly expressing the goodness of nature to which Paul can escape from his industrial home:

'Miriam went on her knees before one cluster, took a wild-looking daffodil between her hands, turned up its face of gold to her, and bowed down caressing it with her mouth and cheeks and brow'.

Her action is sexual yet chaste, loving yet oppressive. It provokes Paul into a cruel denunciation of her possessiveness. ' "You're always begging things to love you" ' he says, ' "as if you were a beggar for love. Even the flowers, you have to fawn on them –" ' (pp. 267–8). The scene thus serves two purposes, on the one hand to show a pastoral world in which Paul can make contact with pleasures unknown in Bestwood, where he lives, but on the other to use this world for explicitly metaphorical purposes. It is an Eden, in which love can be encountered not only as a sexual experience but as something spiritually oppressive, and ultimately life-restricting rather than fulfilling.

Though Miriam is partly based on Jessie Chambers, who was offended by this portrayal of her relationship with Lawrence, she often seems in the novel less a creature of flesh and blood than a 'literary' prototype, platonic and allusive. She creates around herself a nun-like and romantic purity, giving herself to Paul more as an act of self-

37

Jessie Chambers. A portrait taken when she was training to become a teacher. She was among Lawrence's closest friends in his adolescence and early manhood: he drew upon this experience to create the character of Miriam in *Sons and Lovers*.

martyrdom than in a spirit of sexual partnership. Her instincts attract her to figures in history and to saints in paintings. She does not like the reality of known experience so much as the chimeras of fiction, and thus she models her relationship with Paul on ideals rather than allowing it to grow out of true instincts. Just as Paul learns to conceal from his mother all his private feelings which do not directly impinge upon her, so he comes to realize how much of his true self has to be held back in his relationship with Miriam.

Like Lettie in *The White Peacock* Miriam lacks the capacity to grow in harmony with her partner. Paul outstrips her. A modern feminist case against *Sons and Lovers* would centre on the manner in which Lawrence presents the women in the novel only as instruments for Paul's awakening to manhood. The charge does not altogether hold true, however. Miriam is inadequate *in her own right*. By the Lawrentian standard she does not permit her repressed sexuality any kind of natural outlet, so that she can give herself only in an act of self-abnegation. She denies the possibilities in her own life as well as in Paul's. Similarly, Paul's mother, though emotionally very affecting for most readers, never knows a life of give and take in equal proportions. She wants to possess or to dominate or to live through the surrogate satisfaction of other people's achievements.

Clara Dawes comes closest to the modern feminist position by making a free choice to return to her husband after initiating Paul into a fuller manhood than Miriam could ever provide, but Clara's strength contrasts, like Mrs. Morel's and Walter's, with the weakness of her husband. Far from the women of the novel being only staging posts in Paul's progress to adulthood, they loom like intransigent fates who induct him into mysteries only at the threat of extinguishing his personal light. At the end of the novel, when he feels himself 'infinitesimal, at the core of nothingness, and yet not nothing', we do not remember Paul as the thwarter of female aspirations. The women of the novel have shown a strength which, alone now, he has to prove he has himself. In his relationships with women, whether as a son or as a lover, Paul has resisted being taken over. It most nearly happens in the natural bond of mother and son, but Miriam and Clara threaten it in different ways. He resists not just to preserve his personal identity but because the right equation cannot be established between a consuming partner, as Lawrence sees these women, and a still weak man who has not worked out for himself a conduct of being. The feminist argument has some truth in it if it claims that Lawrence makes the women of *Sons and Lovers* tyrannizing and emasculating, but none at all if the case rests on an accusation that they have no being except to feed Paul Morel's vanity.

In his first two novels Lawrence had tried to deal with sexual feeling in a discreet way. Even in *The Trespasser*, the main subject of which is an adulterous passion, he does not often find a language capable of facing the issues head-on. His view of sex sometimes seems more theoretical than intuitive in these early novels, either because of poetic evasions or because of a simple incapacity to talk in a sustained way about sexual feeling. It is therefore astonishing to see how much Lawrence matured as a writer in the few months that separate the final revision of *The Trespasser* in February 1912 and the completion of *Sons and Lovers* in November of the same year. Now when he wants to be poetic the passage does not read as decorative gilding or adolescent extravagance but as a necessary part of the symbolic patterning. Flower imagery is applied with a consciously associative value. Set pieces, like Paul and Miriam beside the ivory-coloured roses (in Chapter 7) or their love-making at the time of the cherry harvest (in Chapter 11), are fully integrated into the novel. Naturalistic dialogue is used to explore feeling in a more direct way than perhaps any English novelist had used it before. Here, for example, are Clara and Paul in Chapter 13.

'Do you think it's worth it – the – the sex part?'
'The act of loving itself?'
'Yes; is it worth anything to you?'
'But how can you separate it?' he said. 'It's the culmination of everything. All our intimacy culminates then.'
'Not for me,' she said. ' . . . I feel,' she continued slowly, 'as if I hadn't got you, as if all of you weren't there, and as if it weren't

me you were taking –'
'Who, then?'
'Something just for yourself. It has been fine, so that I daren't think of it. But is it *me* you want, or is it *It*?' (p. 441)

The passage reads calmly and undramatically, yet it conveys so much that Lawrence struggles to articulate in this novel, but which he had hardly ventured to express in his first two books. What is the relationship of love and sex? Must sexual passion entail possessiveness? Is there a chance of creating a balance between partners? How can the awareness of self in one person be matched by a knowledge of the other person's selfhood? Does the one-ness of me necessarily prevent me from seeing the you-ness of you, and if I see it can I seek it out without wanting to crush it? Are Miriam's self-denial or Paul's self-gratification the only ways in which sexual feeling can express themselves? Lawrence explores personal and sometimes mystical experiences through language that carefully balances ordinary speech with poetic intensification. This, as much as its reputation for emotional honesty, is one of the strengths of this great novel.

Though Lawrence analyzes relationships in *Sons and Lovers* so well, we ought not to forget his success in conveying the detail of late nineteenth-century working life in both a mining and a farming community. The novel moves freely between the two, partly reminding us of how an industrialized village like Bestwood (Lawrence's own hometown, Eastwood) seems like an ugly gash on the landscape. The miners' lives, the petty class distinctions which grow up even in a poor community, the suspicion of books, the attraction of London, the way in which competitions and scholarships provide almost the only avenue of escape for an intelligent young man, all these come fully alive as we read *Sons and Lovers*. Lawrence's self-analysis and his depiction of the halting way in which youth moves into maturity would have far less density and even credibility if the social background were less effectively realized. In *Sons and Lovers* he wrote probably his most immediately approachable book and the one which readers will bother with, even if they cannot tolerate anything else he wrote. If the ability to remind men of their own lives in a way that makes common experiences seem special is the gift of a major writer, then Lawrence proves himself many times in *Sons and Lovers*.

5. *THE RAINBOW*

'I love and adore this new book,' Lawrence wrote in March 1913, ' . . . I think it's great – so new, so really a stratum deeper than I think anybody has ever gone, in a novel.' Though he writes this in the first month of its composition, Lawrence's intention for *The Rainbow* is clear from the start. This was to be a novel not only unlike the three he himself had written ('It is all analytical – quite unlike *Sons and Lovers*, not a bit visualized', he adds in the same letter) but a new departure for the form of the novel itself. There is immense confidence in the way Lawrence talks of this new book, as though he now felt equipped to tackle something on an altogether larger scale than anything he had attempted before, a novel not drawn from personal experience, as basically both *Sons and Lovers* and *The White Peacock* had been, or from the experience of a friend, as *The Trespasser* derived from Helen Corke's affair with Herbert Macartney, but concerned with the way in which modern English society had reached its contemporary state. Indeed, larger than this, Lawrence took nothing less than the evolution of man as his theme. It shocked him profoundly when *The Rainbow* was published in 1915 that it met with a disapproving reception and eventual banning on account of its supposed obscenity.

Lawrence conceived *The Rainbow* and *Women in Love* as one novel. Initially he intended calling this work *The Sisters* and subsequently he refers to it as *The Wedding Ring*, a particularly apt title as the central subject of the book was to be the way in which a complete being might be realized, perfectly in union with their chosen partner and at one with a united society. The ring has conventionally been a symbol of union and perfection: in thinking of *The Wedding Ring*

as a title for his new work Lawrence intimated his wish to write a novel about the potential perfectibility of man. As he worked further on the novel his bright conception seemed to cloud, and eventually he felt he could no longer sustain the vision in a single book. He thus split *The Sisters* or *The Wedding Ring* into *The Rainbow* and *Women in Love*, linking them principally through the character of Ursula Brangwen, but creating in the second novel almost a modifier of the first. The structure of *Women in Love* is quite different from *The Rainbow*, synchronic rather than diachronic (actions happening simultaneously though in different places rather than actions narrated developmentally in a sequence). Though the almost apocalyptic and revelationary images of the first novel carry over into the second, they do so in a less 'plotted' way. Whereas the metaphorical patterning of *The Rainbow* seems at times almost in danger of determining the ideas of the novel rather than of expressing already conceived thoughts, there is an even distribution of arguments in *Women in Love* supported by an intricate network of imagery in which no one symbol prevails over the others. *Women in Love* is the more equivocal novel, though in the end the same vision which inspires *The Rainbow* survives the challenges of powerful counter-visions. Lawrence seems to have found the imaginative life of *The Rainbow* impossible to maintain into a second volume, for his own intellectual honesty demanded that he be fair to the pervasive forces of materialism, capitalism and autocracy which his instincts railed against.

The Rainbow thus has a clarity of utterance which is sometimes less evident in *Women in Love*. It is a saga novel, but so unlike contemporary works like John Galsworthy's *The Forsyte Saga* (1906–21) or Arnold Bennett's *Clayhanger* (1910–16) as to create its own genre within English fiction. The links are with Norse sagas, with the Bible and with *Paradise Lost* if they are anywhere, but Lawrence's achievement is not seriously comparable with these: names and symbols allude to other literatures, some of the language has a Hebraic resonance, but Lawrence does not depend on any imagination but his own to express the nature of his vision.

The Rainbow spans three generations of the Brangwen family. A simplified genealogical plan may help us, with the earliest generation married around 1840.

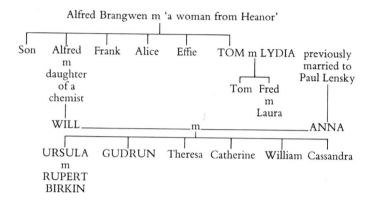

The characters in block capital letters are the principals in *The Rainbow* and *Women in Love*, though Gudrun plays only a minor role in the first novel and Rupert Birkin only appears in the second. Indeed, *Women in Love* concerns the youngest Brangwen generation almost exclusively, Will and Anna having slipped into a passive background and Tom and Lydia being long dead. Though the novels concentrate on the inner lives of these Brangwens, they make their way through a society undergoing such rapid change that this feature itself becomes pivotal to Lawrence's conception. Indeed, the Brangwens in *The Rainbow* have a representational significance, illustrating the movement of solid English farming stock from a wholly agricultural existence to a world in which industrialization and intellectual ambitions have rendered complex and confused their former certainties of belief.

The Rainbow opens with a testament to the lost pre-industrial world. Lawrence knows that history cannot be reversed, though lessons may be learned from it. This world is irrecoverable. It may, nevertheless, be lamented. He therefore writes a prologue to the main novel, though in the guise of an opening chapter, for Lawrence wants the final form of *The Rainbow* to be an organic whole, no part outside the integrated entirety.

In autumn the partridges whirred up, birds in flocks blew like spray across the fallow, rooks appeared on the grey, watery heavens, and flew cawing into the winter. Then the men sat by the fire in the house where the women moved about with surety, and the limbs and the body of the men were impregnated with the day, cattle and earth and vegetation and the sky, the men sat by the fire and their brains were inert, as their blood flowed heavy with the accumulation from the living day. (p. 8)

In a free-flowing, almost impressionistic prose Lawrence establishes an image of pastoral harmony. It is the women who disrupt it.

On them too was the drowse of blood-intimacy, calves sucking and hens running together in droves, and young geese palpitating in the hand while the food was pushed down their throttle. But the women looked out from the heated, blind intercourse of farm-life, to the spoken world beyond. They were aware of the lips and the mind of the world speaking and giving utterance, they heard the sound in the distance, and they strained to listen. (p. 8)

Like Eve, their prototype, the early Brangwen women are not content with their settled existence. They glimpse possibilities of knowledge and material achievement beyond it. Here Lawrence implants in the reader's mind an association – it is no more than that – with the Book of Genesis, and he will loosely move to the Book of Revelations at the end of *Women in Love* when Ursula and Birkin set out to seek a new kind of world; but at no time does he permit his own vision to be moulded by the Biblical parallels. He is more concerned at the start of *The Rainbow* to evoke a pre-industrial world and then to establish within it a conflict of ambitions between the sexes, for this will be the central issue of the novel. The men are content to live this life, the women lust for something more. Lawrence extends the issues upon which the Morel marriage founders in *Sons and Lovers*, but he no longer believes it to be merely a struggle between different kinds of moral perception. The women's behaviour is virtually instinctive, as though at some primeval point when the sexes separated out of the initial life-mass they were imbued with a biological hunger for knowledge and advancement. The first sentence of *The Rainbow* begins 'The Brangwens had lived for generations on the Marsh Farm . . .' as though they have evolved there from the origins of life. Throughout *The Rainbow* and *Women in Love* Lawrence insists on the difference between the sexes as more than obviously physical; it is mental, emotional, within the beings of men and women. 'The man has his pure freedom, the woman hers,' he writes in *Women in Love*. 'Each acknowledges the perfection of the polarized sex-circuit. Each admits the different nature in the other' (p. 225). If this is so, however, does it necessarily mean an inalienable gulf between men and women and an irrevocable isolation for each individual? Lawrence seems anxious to resist such a conclusion. His conviction that the sexes can ideally live in balanced harmony with each other, neither claiming possession of the other (though in reality both often do) is the thesis of both *The Rainbow* and *Women in Love*. Each relationship in the novels explores ways in which such equilibrium may be established, testing the claims of each kind of partnership in an earnest search for proof that the ideal is realizable. Tom and Lydia, Will and Anna, perhaps most positively Ursula and Birkin, show moments of perfected union, though none of these relationships survive without conflict. Lawrence knew from his own marriage that a measure of struggle and argument between both partners was a natural part of a developing relationship, and that once these ceased the union was threatened with extinction. In the various relationships of *The Rainbow* and *Women in Love*, however, he seeks to distinguish between truly creative conflicts and those which, like war, leave only scars and damage.

Tom Brangwen marries Lydia Lensky. He has grown up mainly among women and has a love of poetry and a resentment of 'mechanical stupidity' (p. 16), which separates him from the other Brangwen menfolk of his generation. Lydia is Polish, a stranger in religion and in cast of mind from the community into which she marries. Though Lawrence makes little of her Polishness, using it primarily to convey her 'otherness' or the distance which must always

46

exist between her and Tom, he nonetheless makes no mistakes historically in talking about her background or her first marriage to a failed radical. The details of *The Rainbow* are always accurate and the narrative unfolded with a tight control of chronological accuracy.

Tom and Lydia live in struggle with each other but their marriage is ultimately a success in Lawrence's scheme, for it entails a creative kind of self-questioning and a constant move forward. Lydia's daughter Anna, child of her marriage to Paul Lensky, grows into a wholly self-sufficient person, inheriting her mother's private instincts but none of her giving nature. Anna is one of Lawrence's most original creations. We follow her from her wilful childhood, vexatiously trying to tame the farm geese, to her destructive maturity when she almost voluntarily sloughs her imagination and denies all emotions other than her maternalism. Into her world comes her cousin Will, 'a dark enriching influence she had not known before' (p. 110). The potential is there, Lawrence emphasizes, for a fully balanced partnership, he a worker who can make art and beauty shine out of simple wood, she the begetter of children who has yet glimpsed possibilities of a superior life. 'Something she had not, something she did not grasp, could not arrive at. There was something beyond her. But why must she start on the journey? She stood so safely on the Pisgah mountain' (p. 195). Anna quite literally cannot make the effort to discover the better world which, imaged by the first appearance of a rainbow in the novel, she has been privileged to glimpse: 'She would forfeit it all for the outside things . . . she would throw away the living fruit for the ostensible rind' (p. 151).

There ensues a battle more debilitating than that between the Morels. Will retreats into himself and she finds a limited fulfilment in rearing her children. Theirs, however, is a tragedy of wasted opportunity, for both Will and Anna stifle their own growth. A favourite image of Lawrence's is the plant struggling for life above ground only to meet a stone which causes it to twist itself into a half-formed distortion. It can be applied to Will and Anna, who have the capacity to form the kind of balanced relationship which

47

Lawrence seeks to express, but who turn away from this into an existence of destructive conflict and eventual sterility. Even their moments of reconciliation are self-absorbed, as though opting out of the flow of life.

In their eldest child Ursula Lawrence invests the best possibility of creating a new form of life, for she remains always enquiring and, in *The Rainbow* at least, unfettered. 'Out of nothingness and the undifferentiated mass, to make something of herself!' (p. 283). Her path is partly an intellectual one, partly sexual, but unlike her mother she accepts her destiny as 'a traveller on the face of the earth . . . ultimately and finally, she must go on and on, seeking the goal that she knew she did draw nearer to' (p. 417). At times Lawrence seems to echo Charlotte Brontë's imagery in *Jane Eyre* (though in his essay 'Pornography and Obscenity', 1929, he calls this novel 'slightly obscene' on account of Rochester's need to be emasculated before he is worthy of Jane) – he speaks of Ursula as a bird, an infant crying in the night, a moon-person whose reality is not wholly of this world. Yet her first attempts to make sense of her life are through dedicated service to society. Her days as a schoolteacher show her something of the intractability of human nature and they allow Lawrence an opportunity to write with scathing accuracy about the English classrooms of his own day wherein educational ideals almost inevitably fall victim to expediency.

In a perhaps conscious allusion to *Jane Eyre* Ursula has the opportunity to leave England and go to India. Her relationship with the Polish aristocrat Skrebensky, like Jane's with St. John Rivers, has an almost comic edge to it, for it is wholly out of balance. He is a son of institutional life, restricted by class, by the army, by his code of propriety. She triumphs over him not as Anna triumphs over Will, exulting in being the 'Anna Victrix' of Chapter 6, but because she is simply too free and too large to be partnered with him for any significant length of time. Skrebensky is a stage in her personal and sexual development, but in the end no more relevant to her fulfilment than her lesbian attraction towards a fellow schoolteacher. Ursula's true consummation comes in *Women in Love*, when it takes almost a mystical and transfiguring form. Lawrence in *The Rainbow* shows the limitations as well as the glories of sexuality.

The Rainbow is five-hundred pages long, densely and often poetically written. Occasionally this awareness of its own scale leads to some falseness of vision – the final manifestation of the rainbow, though beautiful in rhythm and tone, surely sacrifices truth to symbol, as though Lawrence felt he must end on a high prophetic note when the argument of the novel calls for an open-ended, speculative, anxious conclusion. The novel cannot be satisfactorily summarized in a few pages, but one can be reasonably certain that nowhere else in English fiction does a writer come so close to embodying in his characters the main tensions of industrialized man or the issues which at once separate and bind the sexes.

6. *WOMEN IN LOVE*

In one of his best argued and most persuasive chapters in *D. H. Lawrence: Novelist* F. R. Leavis says of *Women in Love*:

> Even a reader who is still far from having grasped the full thematic development must be aware by the time he reaches the end of the book that it contains a presentation of twentieth-century England – of modern civilization – so first-hand and searching in its comprehensiveness as to be beyond the powers of any other novelist he knows of. (p. 155)

Here is the immediate difference between *Women in Love* and *The Rainbow*. Its vigorous contemporaneity contrasts with the more grandiose conception of *The Rainbow*, where Lawrence seems at times to be hampered by the lofty symbolism. Though there is a great deal of explicit social detail in *The Rainbow* it does not convey so specific a sense of period as *Women in Love*, with its café society, its smart observation of clothes and décor, its ear for fashionable nuances and its foreboding of a threat even to the tarnished civilization that modern man has provided for himself.

49

At the start of the last section I drew attention to the initial conception whereby Lawrence envisaged *The Rainbow* and *Women in Love* as one novel. Relics of this remain in the second novel, even though its basic structure fundamentally differs from the first. Lawrence originally intended a saga of man's history from the marshes (hence the name of the Brangwen farm) out of which life evolved up to the present corruptible moment – and beyond that to a future where he will either have established a viable society quite different from the one he now inhabits, or have ceased to exist at all. The latter proposition is seriously countenanced in *Women in Love*, mainly in what Birkin says, though it may be thought that Gerald Crich's materialistic juggernaut is heading for man's extinction too. Birkin does not want to see the end of the human race, but he does not believe it to be either inconceivable or totally disastrous.

'Let mankind pass away – time it did. The creative utterances will not cease, they will only be there. Humanity doesn't embody the utterance of the incomprehensible any more. Humanity is a dead letter. There will be a new embodiment, in a new way. Let humanity disappear as quickly as possible.' (p. 65)

Lawrence by now has arrived at a religious conviction which he never forsook. It has pantheistic elements, but it is too personally felt and totally uninstitutionalized to be given a recognized conceptual name. He sees in the universe a 'primal sympathy – which having been must ever be': Wordsworth's words come close to expressing it. This creative presence informs all nature; man is only a detail, more complex than most but not on this account indispensable to the universe. More than once the novel reminds us of the demise of certain mammals, which evolution regarded as expendable. Man may go the way of the dinosaur. If so, the universal force will not die. There will still, in a famous image of the novel, be hares sitting up in empty fields.

Lawrence's romantic vision is presented in some of his most high-sounding but ultimately unsatisfactory prose, for it convinces more by rhetoric and poetic diction than by intelligence. Many times in *Women in Love* we have to be on our guard against Lawrence's compulsive language, for it sometimes argues a point of view contrary to the general direction of the novel. Birkin's speeches on the irrelevance of man to the cosmic scheme exemplify this. Phrases like 'Let mankind pass away – time it did' and 'Humanity is a dead letter' no doubt express Lawrence's own feelings in certain moods, but they do not satisfactorily indicate the beliefs of the novel, though they come dangerously close to diverting the reader from Lawrence's central conviction that life *is* worth living, that it must survive and that a world without man would be as good as inert; however dynamic the energies which continued to inform it, a globe devoid of humanity would have no vision to perceive it or consciousness to absorb it. It would be living, but it might as well be dead. Lawrence's faith in man, however monstrously wrong the paths he has taken, never profoundly deserts him. It is a weakness of *Women in Love* that we so often worry that it may be about to do so. This is what Leavis means when he talks of places in the novel where 'Lawrence betrays by an insistent and over-emphatic explicitness, running at times to something one can only call jargon, that he is uncertain – uncertain of the value of what he offers; uncertain whether he really holds it' (*D. H. Lawrence: Novelist*, p. 155).

Women in Love is a novel of ideas, though paradoxically one of its main ideas contends that the world suffers too much from thought and intellect. Indeed, there are points in the book (*pace* the late plays of Samuel Beckett) where Lawrence almost comes to reject language because it is the instrument of cerebral experiences. Birkin expresses this in a passage when we feel he is not negating the main flow of the novel, as in his speech quoted earlier, but reaching for a means of saying something which is verbally almost inexpressible. He is speaking to Ursula.

'There is,' he said, in a voice of pure abstraction, 'a final one which is stark and impersonal and beyond responsibility. So there is a final you. And it is there I would want to meet you – not in the emotional, loving plane – but there beyond, where there is no speech and no terms of agreement. There we are two stark, unknown beings, two utterly strange creatures, I would want to approach you, and you me. And there could be no obligation, because there is no standard for action there, because no understanding has been reaped from that plane. It is quite inhuman – so there can be no calling to book, in any form whatsoever – because one is outside the pale of all that is accepted, and nothing known applies. One can only follow the impulse, taking that which lies in front, and responsible for nothing, asked for nothing, giving nothing, only each taking according to the primal desire.' (pp. 162–3)

Here is the kernel not only of *Women in Love* but of all Lawrentian fiction. Characteristically the truest moments in his prose totally lack rhetoric. This flows naturalistically, like real speech rather than speech-making. Birkin advocates a meeting of the sexes without the restrictions of morality or custom, the setting up of a new world which quite literally starts afresh. All that language has rationalized and 'terms of agreement' defined will be made redundant. It is useless to ask what practically Lawrence means by this: how will such a society be established, where will it operate, how can it preserve privacy? He is writing almost allegorically of the *need* for a better world where the achievements of clever men will not automatically be regarded as the right criteria for human life. He appeals, in other words, for an opportunity whereby the emotional depths in men and women can be allowed to surface. We need not be the slaves of self-restraint.

Ursula aspires to this personal freedom throughout *Women in Love*. 'Her spirit was active, her life like a shoot that is growing steadily, but which has not yet come above ground' (p. 57). Within an immensely complex novel Lawrence shows not only Ursula but several other characters striving for personal attainments. Her sister Gudrun sees her own salvation within the sophisticated world. Gerald Crich sees it in the triumph of the machine-based society. Both of them wish to discipline their lives, to impose curbs upon natural feeling and to see enforced a set of absolute values which will test men and thus weed out the weak from the strong. Theirs is an anti-life belief because it denies nature. We see it most dramatically expressed in the scene where Gudrun exults as Gerald cruelly tries to tame his mare. Eventually Gudrun deserts Gerald in favour of the industrial

Lamb Close House. The home of the Barber family, the owners for several generations of the Eastwood Collieries. The house is described in *The White Peacock* and again as the home of the Crich family in *Women in Love* and as Wragby Hall in *Lady Chatterley's Lover*. *Warren Roberts and Laurence Pollinger Ltd.*

Moorgreen Reservoir. In *The White Peacock* and *Sons and Lovers* this is known as Nethermere. In *Women in Love* it is called Willey Water, the scene of the boating party and the drowning of Gerald Crich's sister. *Keith Sagar*

artist Loerke who, in the final chapters of the novel, epitomizes the separation of art from life and of reason from instinct.

Lawrence's attitude to Gerald Crich demonstrates his humanity as a novelist. 'This is the first and finest state of chaos', says Lawrence of Gerald's beliefs, 'pure organic disintegration and pure mechanical organization' (p. 260). Everything which Gerald stands for repels Lawrence, yet his portrait moves us greatly, almost as Milton's Satan makes us weep in pity. Gerald and his father worship the machine, as though it can protect them against a knowledge of death. Terror lies at the centre of their beings. They therefore seek power over men, animals, land and objects, for without it they would topple into the dark abyss. They know no inner life, whereas Ursula and Birkin struggle to release theirs.

Birkin and Gerald are powerfully attracted to each other, and there can be little doubt, if one reads the Prologue to *Women in Love* which Lawrence decided to keep back from publication, that the relationship was meant to encompass homosexual feeling. This is not presented with any trace of eroticism, but as one possible means by which men might know each other better. The possibility of love between men (or between women, as suggested in *The Rainbow*) does not appal Lawrence, because he believes it need not exclude the love of men for women. Nor by this is he appealing for bisexuality in men, but the capacity to love in a brotherly way (this may include touch, hence the wrestling scene in the novel, but not homosexual intercourse) even while one loves a person of the opposite sex. Birkin reaches for a relationship with Gerald at the same time that he moves forward with Ursula: the two relationships need not be mutually exclusive and it would, of course, be absurd to talk of them as promiscuous.

Women in Love, as Leavis implies, presents a picture of contemporary England. Sometimes this can be seen in its satirical portraiture – Bertrand Russell and Ottoline Morrell (the famous society hostess) are two of the victims, the latter comically parodied in the extravagant Hermione. On a larger scale, however, Lawrence indicts the capitalist ethos of post-Edwardian England. He does not adopt a socialist or radical stance by which to do this, but portrays working-class existence as demeaning and mechanistic. The problem, however, is that he offers no alternative to it. When Ursula and Birkin go off to seek their own fulfilment they have to do so outside any social context. Lawrence himself wandered away from industrialized society in the years following the writing of *Women in Love*, as we shall explore in the next sections of this study, but he fails to realize that this option simply does not exist for most people.

At the end of the novel, literally in its closing lines, the debate about society and personal freedom continues. *Women in Love* is, like most of Lawrence's major fiction, open-ended and uncommitted when it finishes. Ursula and Birkin wander off, uncertain what they will make of the future. Gudrun and Loerke represent all the life-denying forces which, after Lawrence's own death in 1930, were to manifest themselves in Nazism. Gerald has died, crushed by the forces of nature (symbolically represented by a glacier) which he always tried to control. The novel is about exploring life, but not about reaching destinations. English literature has subsequently had other examples of this technique whereby the author does not seek to express certainties or to define absolutes, but *Women in Love* in its own time created a new form of fiction because it did not move towards a settled conclusion or seek to leave a comprehensive overview in the mind of the reader.

In 1925 Lawrence wrote an essay entitled 'Reflections on the Death of a Porcupine' in which he describes an incident when he shot a porcupine. The episode illustrates the natural balance of the world: 'the whole of creation is established upon the fact that one life devours another life, one cycle of existence can only come into existence through the subjugation of another cycle of existence, then what is the good of trying to pretend that it is not so?' The passage neatly indicates that Lawrence was not a sentimentalist. Nature is rough and it presupposes the superiority of some creatures over others. At the time he wrote the essay, contemporary with *The Plumed Serpent*, Lawrence no doubt assumed that some men were naturally higher in the cycle of existence than some others. It provides an interesting retrospective view of *Women in Love*, for as an essay 'Reflections on the Death of a Porcupine' shows that a certain amount of callousness and aggression are endemic to nature. *Women in Love* shares this view but it indicates, often through examples of human mastery over animals (a cuttle-fish, a mare, a rabbit), but also through attempts by one man to subjugate another, that the natural balance can easily be overturned by excess – by delight in cruelty, by greed and by exploitation of others. Though the novel will strike many readers as Lawrence's most intellectual achievement (despite its wish to depose intellectual gods), it resounds with this deep humanity that deplores any kind of behaviour which imbalances nature. Accept the savagery that must exist within nature as one accepts death as the end of life, but do not add to it. Gerald and Gudrun go too far, Ursula and Birkin draw back. *Women in Love* is less a novel about opposites than about checks and balances.

7. *THE LOST GIRL*

It is not uncommon for great writers to reach a point of creative exhaustion following the completion of a major work. This certainly happened to D. H. Lawrence who, after finishing *Women in Love*, seriously contemplated abandoning the writing of fiction, perhaps in favour of speculative essays, more book-reviewing, translations (he became fascinated with the Sicilian novelist Giovanni Verga) and poems. He had not recovered from the reception given to *The Rainbow* and seriously questioned the value of writing unappreciated novels. 'I feel I don't want to write – still less do I want to publish anything. It is like throwing one's treasures in a bog', he declared in April 1919. It was during this period, when he felt so directionless, that Lawrence wrote *The Lost Girl*, a novel which fundamentally changes its character as it develops. Lawrence starts it as though he were trying to concede ground to critics who had resented his lack of conventionality. In the first half of *The Lost Girl* he does not complicate his realistic portrait of the English lower middle-class with sexual radicalism or metaphysics. We might almost be reading a novel by John Galsworthy or Arnold Bennett. There are, too, strong echoes of Dickens, particularly of *Hard Times* in the episodes with the travelling vaudevillians, the absurdly named Natcha-Kee-Tawaras. Yet in the second part of the novel Lawrence seems released from these restraints and finds his own voice. The novel moves to Italy, the relationships become more sexually explicit, a hankering for non-urbanized living creeps in.

This almost abrupt change of emphasis used to be attributed to a gap in the composition of the novel, it being assumed that the first part was written before 1914 when Lawrence left the manuscript in Germany and the second half after 1918 when he was able to take it up again. Keith Sagar, however, in his recent book *D. H. Lawrence: A Calendar of His Works* (1979), has challenged this suggestion, and indicated that the whole of *The Lost Girl* was written after the war. If so, it means that the shifts of view within the novel were planned from the outset. Alternatively, and more probably, Lawrence embarked on this novel with the intention of making it more like the kind of fiction his popular contemporaries were writing, but his natural form of self-expression made it impossible for him to complete the book in such a cut-and-dried manner. As he wrote in his essay on John Galsworthy (1928), defending by implication his own tendency not to be straight-jacketed by conventions of morality or technique.

'If life is a great highway, then it must forge on ahead into the unknown . . . The tip of the road is always unfinished, in the wilderness . . . In the three early novels . . . it looked as if Mr. Galsworthy might break through the blind end of the highway with the dynamite of satire, and help us on to a new lap. But the sex ingredient of his dynamite was damp and muzzy, the explosion gradually fizzled off into sentimentality . . .'

My belief is that Lawrence found his own writing in the middle stages of *The Lost Girl* becoming 'damp and muzzy' and that the re-direction of the novel was a consequence of his need to preserve his sense of his own artistic integrity.

Lawrence contemplated several titles for *The Lost Girl*, each one indicating something of its theme. In its earliest form, the one which Sagar says Lawrence began before the war but subsequently scrapped, it was called *The Insurrection of Miss Houghton*. Later on he thought of *Mixed Marriage*, *Perdition* and *The Bitter Cherry* as possible titles. The novel concerns Alvina Houghton, a respectably brought-up draper's daughter in a town called Woodhouse. She rejects the conventional world in which she is reared by trying several paths of escape – as a nurse in London, as a pianist in her father's cinema, and as the lover of an inarticulate vaudeville artist called Francesco Marasca, 'Cicio'. Cicio's surname derives from a kind of cherry, just as 'Alvina' relates to the Italian word for 'womb' (*alvo*). Lawrence often intended us to pick up hints from the naming of his characters, more because of their associations than for what they specifically mean. In *The Lost Girl* the links between the cherry and the womb indicate the strong sexual theme upon which the novel centres. Alvina finds in the dark magnetic Italian artist a quality of being which is absolutely unknown in damp repressed Woodhouse. In the last chapters of the book she goes with Cicio to a mountain village in southern Italy, but Lawrence does not provide the banal and sentimental conclusion which a romantic escapist would offer. Life for Alvina becomes harder as Cicio returns to his enclosed world of male comradeship and strong family ties, but she refuses to be crushed by it. At the end of the novel (which, surely taking something from the pre-1914 first version, is set on the eve of the war) Alvina contemplates a future in America, the 'New World' with her Italian soul-mate.

The English novel has many examples of main characters awakening to a new consciousness of life. Nineteenth-century convention did not altogether disguise the sexual implication in this. Anne Elliot in *Persuasion*, Jane Eyre, Jude the Obscure, all have to come to terms with their own sexuality. Lawrence handles this subject without inhibition, but whereas in Paul Morel and Ursula Brangwen he presents the sexual aspect as only one part of a carefully balanced equation in their personalities – they are as con-

cerned with finding the right kind of society for themselves –
in Alvina Houghton's case the flowering of her sexual self
is the mainstream of the novel. We understand this early
in the book when she goes down her father's mine, an
unGalsworthian interruption among the first chapters:

There was a thickness in the air, a sense of dark, fluid presence
in the thick atmosphere, the dark, fluid, viscous voice of the
collier making a broad-vowelled, clapping sound in her ear. He
seemed to linger near her as if he knew – as if he knew – what?
Something forever unknowable and inadmissible, something
that belonged purely to the underground: to the slaves who
worked underground: knowledge humiliated, subjected, but
ponderous and inevitable . . . She felt herself melting out also,
to become a mere vocal ghost, a presence in the thick atmosphere. Her lungs felt thick and slow, her mind dissolved, she
felt she could cling like a bat in the long swoon of the crannied,
underworld darkness. (p. 64)

This is a totally different way of writing about the mines
from that of *Sons and Lovers*. Lawrence hardly seems
interested in the work going on or in the economic state
of the mine. It exists as a means of exploring Alvina's inner
being, the self we have not had revealed in the early more
socially descriptive chapters. Alvina yearns to subjugate her
Woodhouse being and become a reborn person. When she
meets Cicio, the means of achieving this rebirth, she changes
her name and becomes Allaye, as though disposing of one
identity to allow the free flow of another. She is 'the lost
girl' because she loses her own self to release a new person.

    Alvina is 'lost' in the different sense of being no longer
acceptable to the prim society of her upbringing. In his
correspondence at the time of writing *The Lost Girl*
Lawrence sometimes refers to it as 'a rather comic novel'.
We ought to remember this when we read about the
adventures of Mr. Houghton, a man of grandly impractical
schemes, of the pinched Miss Pinnegar, the fussy Mr. May,
the hysterical Mrs. Tuke and the theatrical Madame
Rochard, who governs the Natcha-Kee-Tawara troupe.
Each one is a comic *vignette* of considerable style. Together
they form a Dickensian world which hovers on the edge of
caricature, but the satirical humour with which Lawrence

endows them helps to temper the passionate relationship of Alvino and Cicio at the centre of the book. Since the novel lacks the semi-autobiographical pain of *Sons and Lovers* or the marvellous proliferation of ideas which well beneath the action of *The Rainbow* and *Women in Love*, we need this comic detail to focus the intense main theme.

In *The Lost Girl* Lawrence makes an effective study of English provincial attitudes towards the foreigner. Cicio seems exotic and animal-like in the context of Woodhouse, but ordinary and even sad in his own village of Pescocalascio. He says very little in the novel. His presence is felt more than observed. Lawrence suggests that Cicio is inscrutable, that he cannot altogether be summarized as Latinate and foreign or be nearly contrasted as Alvina's physical opposite and instrument of her sexual liberation. He has an 'otherness', a mystery resulting not from the author's lack of interest in his subject but from his deliberate intention to create a character who cannot be fully described. In this respect Lawrence, who introduces Cicio quite late in the novel, is experimenting with the possibilities of characterization in fiction. Having begun *The Lost Girl* in a more orthodox way than in any of his previous stories, he ends up by trying to portray a character whose nature partly defies rational description or conventional psychological analysis. He takes this attempt further in *The Plumed Serpent*, particularly with Don Cipriano, but his next three novels were to be set either entirely or predominantly outside England, as though he was interested in exploring the nature of foreignness itself. *The Lost Girl* is a bridging novel, but in its own right it ought not to be underestimated, for its mixture of comic observation and exoticism makes it one of Lawrence's most easily read and entertaining works of fiction.

8. *AARON'S ROD*

And the Lord spake unto Moses, saying . . . And it shall come to pass, that the man's rod, whom I shall choose, shall blossom . . . And it came to pass, that on the morrow Moses went into the tabernacle of witness; and, behold, the rod of Aaron for the house of Levi was budded, and brought forth buds, and bloomed blossoms, and yielded almonds.

(The Book of Numbers, Ch. 17, vv. 1, 5, 8)

Aaron's Rod (1922) is a novel about flowering in a strange land. Its main character, Aaron Sisson, lives in the same kind of domestic dullness as Siegmund in *The Trespasser* and, like him, he earns his living by playing in an orchestra. The first chapter drily describes the bitterness into which Aaron's marriage and home life have sunk. 'The acute familiarity of his house, which he had built for his marriage twelve years ago, the changeless pleasantness of it all seemed unthinkable. It prevented his thinking' (p.19). In *The Trespasser* the hero escapes from this sort of life by committing adultery and then by killing himself. Neither solution pleased Lawrence, for whatever the strains a marriage might create he did not admire infidelity. The only other major example of it in his work is Lady Chatterley's, though her 'adultery' with Mellors is more by way of attaining a fulfilment which her husband can neither physically nor emotionally supply. As for suicide, we have already seen that Lawrence regarded it as solving nothing. It was an escape *from* life, but not *into* life. In *Aaron's Rod*, however, he begins to examine the possibility that fulfilment may be attained not through sexual means so much as by submission to a dominant person or idea.

Aaron leaves his home and goes to London. Here he encounters Rawdon Lilly, a compulsive philosophiser who befriends him and nurses him back to health when he falls ill. The portrait of Lilly is probably based on John Middleton Murry, the critic and personal friend of Lawrence. Elements of the young Mussolini possibly colour the characterisation in the Italian chapters of the book, because Lawrence observed at first hand the beginnings of Fascism and heard some of the hectic speeches which accompanied them. Aaron follows Lilly across Europe and at the end of the novel supports such an act of abasement. As Lilly puts it, 'there must be one who urges, and one who is impelled' (p. 346). He states this as though it were a natural law like those which govern magnetism and gravity.

This thesis of submission by the weak to the strong is a serious attempt by Lawrence to find a way of establishing harmony between human beings. Instead of competition and struggle we should seek for the right balance between people, in sex, in politics, in religion. It fails to convince, however, because Lilly is simply not interesting enough to sustain the role demanded of him by Lawrence. We have to take on trust his charismatic effect upon Aaron. What he actually says and does in the novel is too often bombastic and sometimes confusing. Some critics, therefore, have tried to find a homosexual element in the Aaron-Lilly relationship, but if it is there, as implicitly it may be, it must detract from what Lawrence is centrally asserting, for his point in *Aaron's Rod* is not primarily sexual. He claims that a better balance will be struck in the world if the mass submit to the benevolent will of great leaders. In the early 1920's when Fascism had not yet been seriously politically tested, this notion appealed to many people, but Lawrence fails to represent it credibly because his embodiment of the leadership impulse lacks intellectual dynamism. Lilly is essentially undistinguished, lacking even the remote other-worldliness of Cicio in *The Lost Girl*.

Though Lawrence himself led a peripatetic life from 1919 onwards and reflected this in his writing he did not produce any other work as unrooted as *Aaron's Rod*. While its title and central metaphor betokens wandering, the novel is wholly concerned with unsettled people. Aaron's companions in London and in Italy are fashionable dilettantes, who might as easily have come from the pages of an early Evelyn Waugh novel. Indeed, most of them are based on actual people. Lawrence laughs at them, but without humour. They are butterflies flitting across the surface of Europe, and we can therefore expect little seriousness from them. *Aaron's Rod* is in some ways a tantalizing novel since it raises the spectre of deracinated intellectuals abandoning England because it is philistine or because they feel sexually

Lawrence in 1920.   *Radio Times Hulton Picture Library*

incompatible with its moral climate or simply because they prefer an alternative culture: but it makes little of this theme, even though such a situation was obviously close to Lawrence's own predicament. In his other 'travel' novels, *Kangaroo* and *The Plumed Serpent*, he places the wanderer in a context: primeval Australia, Aztec Mexico. In *Aaron's Rod* all the characters seem caught in a vortex relating to nothing outside itself. By setting the novel mainly in London and Florence, Lawrence has the opportunity to create a context for his analysis of leadership and disillusionment, but he avoids it. He provides a civilized setting for his story, only to miss its significance.

Aaron's Rod has never been particularly popular among Lawrence's novels. This may be because it is alone among his works in having no prominent female character. The most characteristically Lawrentian element is therefore missing, the assessment of relationships between the sexes. It was probably a necessary novel for him to have written at the most uncertain period of his life when he was deciding where his future lay, but it is the closest he came to an aesthetic failure. He wrote it in bits, beginning it in November 1917 and not completing it until June 1921. This shows, for the novel has no coherent imaginative design. It allowed him, however, to experiment with an episodic fictional structure and to try out some ideas which he developed more fully in his next book. *Kangaroo*, an altogether more successful novel, capitalizes on the looseness of form and woolliness of thinking which afflict *Aaron's Rod*, making strengths out of their weakness. If Aaron's rod brings forth any blossom at all, then it flowers in *Kangaroo*.

9. *KANGAROO*

Lawrence's decision to leave England had been intimated in his correspondence and had been detectable, so some of his contemporaries realized, in aspects of *Women in Love*, *The Lost Girl* and *Aaron's Rod*, but it was only on 26 February 1922 that he and Frieda embarked at Naples for his first voyage outside Europe. They called briefly at Ceylon but their destination was intentionally – and perhaps symbolically – as far from Britain as possible. It is perhaps important to remember how comparatively unknown the Antipodes were in the early 1920's to most British people: legends of Ned Kelly and Rolf Boldrewood's novels of hardy outdoor life (the most famous of which is *Robbery Under Arms*) encouraged a notion of Australia as the antithesis of English suburbia. Lawrence hoped to discover there a kind of pre-civilization where men, learning by the mistakes of the northern European, would in effect have begun again. He was not to find this 'ur-society' among Australian men or women and he did not make contact with aboriginal Australia, as he would surely have wanted to do had he been visiting it now, but he did discover in the landscape of the outback a scale in nature grander than anything he had seen before, and hence, in his estimation, close to the well-springs of the universe. Trim England, even the wildness of Cornwall, could not compete with the essence of un-restraint which 'the pale, white unwritten atmosphere of Australia' had upon Lawrence. It resulted in writing about which it is difficult to talk without evoking a paradox, for it is at once coolly objective and yet wholly passionate:

To be alone, mindless and memoryless between the sea, under the sombre wall-front of Australia. To be alone with a long, wide shore and land, heartless, soulless. As alone and as absent and as present as an aboriginal dark on the sand in the sun. The strange falling-away of everything. (p. 365)

Lawrence's descriptions of landscape in *Kangaroo* are among the best he wrote outside his travel books, and even today many native-born Australian writers fall short of them. His account of the humanity which inhabits this preternatural setting does not have the same concentration: instead of a successfully paradoxical style Lawrence veers confusingly between extremes of emotion. *Kangaroo* is his most autobiographical novel in that he wrote it whilst experiencing the events from which the novel takes its life. The autobiographical elements in his other novels, including *Sons and Lovers*, are recollections in comparative tranquillity.

65

In *Kangaroo* the writing of the novel often reflects what Lawrence was doing that day, how he felt about Australia, and on what terms he was with his wife, for all but the last chapter of the novel was written during the months of June and July 1922 when he and Frieda stayed in New South Wales. The book thus allows us a unique chance to see Lawrence's volatility transmuted into his prose. The shapelessness of the novel, verging occasionally on incoherence, has led the majority of critics to label it a failure, but it is pertinent to wonder whether any other form would have conveyed so much immediacy of reaction. Chapter 8 of *Kangaroo* is called 'Volcanic Evidence' and Chapter 14 is called 'Bits', headings which sum up Lawrence's intention in this novel not to give a fully-rounded interpretation of the Australia he visited but something more exploratory, more rough-hewn and more like the experience of life as we actually feel it.

Richard and Harriet Somers come to Australia like strangers, a point emphasized in the amusing first pages of *Kangaroo* when the 'Aussie' workmen speculate whether they might be 'Fritzies' or 'Bolshies'. This is post-first world war society but the prejudices remain. Indeed, the moulding influence of 1914–18 can scarcely be overstated in connection with this novel. It comes to the fore most obviously in Chapter 12, 'Nightmare'. Here the Somers's recall the indignities of life in England during the war and the reasons for their disillusionment with western society. 'No man who has really consciously lived through this can believe again absolutely in democracy' (p. 240), Lawrence writes. His 'Nightmare' chapter is a crucial, though very often unregarded analysis of his reasons for leaving England in search of a better society. The people of England had voluntarily subjected themselves to the mass hysteria, as he saw it, of patriotism, to authoritarianism masquerading as democracy. The war for Lawrence was the obscene culmination of industrialization and science – the tyranny of the mechanical over the natural. Though several poets, most famously Wilfred Owen, had alerted the British public to the horrors of trench warfare, a deep-seated revulsion at how the war had been managed, and particularly how the

66

ordinary people had reacted to the chauvinism of their leaders, had not yet set in. Lawrence was in this respect ahead of his contemporaries in making known his bitterness before it became fashionable to do so.

We hear so much of the bravery and horrors of the front. Brave the men were, all honour to them. It was at home the world was lost. We hear too little of the collapse of the proud human spirit at home, the triumph of sordid, rampant, raging meanness. 'The bite of a jackal is blood-poisoning and mortification.' And at home stayed all the jackals, middle-aged, male and female jackals. And they bit us all. And blood-poisoning and mortification set in. (p. 241)

Such writing bears out Lawrence's comment in a letter when mid-way in creating *Kangaroo* – 'the Lord alone knows what anybody will think of it: no love at all, and attempt at revolution.' He was describing more than just the plot but also the spirit of the book.

Lawrence's own decision to go abroad, dramatized in that of Richard Somers, grew directly out of his conviction that England was dead. As the Somers's leave the coast of England they see it 'like a grey, dreary-grey coffin sinking in the sea behind' (p. 286). Lawrence used this image more than once in his fiction and it presumably captures his funereal feelings as he and Frieda set sail from England in 1919 on the travels that would eventually take them to Australia. In 'Nightmare' we trace the source of this bitterness in one of the least-known but most trenchant pieces of anti-war writing in modern fiction.

The Australia to which the Somers's come is riddled with political dissension. *Kangaroo* has sometimes been cited as a novel in which Lawrence indicated Fascist tendencies. After the failures of 'democracy' in the war many intellectuals felt the need for tighter political leadership, providing it was based on an ability to heal the dissensions in society. Critics of Lawrence such as Bertrand Russell, who accused him of setting out on a path leading to Auschwitz, overlook the novelist's constant tendency to self-reappraisal. In *Kangaroo*, and again in *The Plumed Serpent*, Lawrence has by the end of the book reached a point where he is rejecting charismatic autocracy. The novel considers it seriously, and examines too the claims of the trades-unions on the left, but at no point can Lawrence seriously be seen as a precursor of the Fascism of the 1930's, with its determination to perfect the machinery of society, or of Soviet-style Communism under Stalin. He poses for his readers a problem of discrimination, for he was genuinely attracted by the notion that mankind would only be able to see its way out of its current malaise if it followed the guidance of a great leader, but he also saw how easily this could lead to perversions of power and to the possibility that people would then surrender the last vestiges of their individualism. If Lawrence saw the seductive side of absolute political movements, he was also a prophet of their evils.

Bea Cooley and Willie Struthers are the two leaders around whom Lawrence debates the merits of individual and mass action. Cooley is the 'Kangaroo' of the novel's title, conceived lovingly, associated often with flowers, the phoenix, fire and Christ, as though filled with goodness and life. Yet this born leader of men closes his mind to views different from his own. His message to the world is one of love and hope for change, but it verges on threat. Somers's disillusionment grows stronger and he finally denies *Kangaroo* a death-bed reconciliation. The novel ends in doubt and self-confusion as the Somers's leave Australia. The new country has not offered them the political revelations or the social developments they hoped to find there, though as a time to take stock of each other, to see primeval and suburban worlds in contact, and to become more positively directed towards spiritual regeneration when political and social impulses have failed them, the Australian weeks have been essential. On his last day Somers reflects 'that one of his souls would stand forever out on those rocks beyond the jetty' (p. 391) and so it was for Lawrence, who, in a letter dated 22 June 1922, wrote that 'Australia would be a lovely country to lose the world in altogether'. At no point in his life, however, could Lawrence make such a remark approvingly. He was too concerned to find the world to delight in the possibility of losing it.

Lawrence's travels to Mexico took him among stranger human relics than he had ever seen before. If in Sicily he had glimpsed the possibilities of an ancient civilization surviving in an even more ancient physical setting and in Australia witnessed the conjunction of a primeval landscape with vulgar suburban encroachments, in Mexico he saw not only scenes of undisturbed beauty but the evidence of a religious revival. Mexico, he believed, was regenerating itself. At the time when Lawrence stayed there the country was racked by a dispute between Church and State which broke out into open conflict in the same year that *The Plumed Serpent* was published. The expulsion of Christian images from the churches and the revival of dance-rites in honour of the ancestral gods actually took place as he describes them in the novel. The religion of Quetzalcoatl (whose name is a compound of Aztec words meaning 'plumed serpent') had been a great unifying myth in ancient Mexico. There are different versions of the legend, but undoubtedly Lawrence knew about the religion in detail and was not – as a few critics have supposed him to be doing – weaving a spurious fantasy of his own. He was attracted to the Quetzalcoatl myth because it dealt only in the present, asserting life and rebirth and seeming to deny the finality of death. As Don Ramón puts it in the novel, 'There is no Before and After, there is only Now.' Its symbol was the phoenix, which Lawrence adopted as his own (it appeared on his grave in France before his ashes were removed to New Mexico). He hoped that in the revival of faith he saw at work in Mexico there might exist a viable formula for mankind as a whole.

Lawrence was forty years old when he wrote *The Plumed Serpent*, the same age as Kate Leslie, its main character. Like her, he was torn between abandoning Europe for ever by settling amongst an unsophisticated community, or returning there where he knew his cultural roots would always be. We know from his correspondence at the time that Lawrence felt exactly as Kate does about Mexico when he first went there, and that the minor characters at the start of the novel – Owen, Villiers, Mrs. Norris, for example –

were based on Mabel Sterne and her associates with whom Lawrence frequently stayed. The character of the novel changes, however, when he introduces Don Ramón and Don Cipriano, the two main advocates of the Quetzalcoatl revival.

Lawrence does not entirely resolve the problem of how to make Ramón and Cipriano credible as human beings when they spend so much of their time adopting the *personae* of Aztec deities, Ramón as Quetzalcoatl himself, Cipriano as the war-god Huìtzilopochtli. Ramón seems especially remote from real experience, for Lawrence expects him to be the repository of an enlightened philosophy, a kindly parent and, at least with his second wife Teresa, a loving husband, whilst at the same time he exacts bloody retribution on those who defy Quetzalcoatl, he drives his wife Carlota to her death, and he participates in strange ceremonies of invocation to the Morning Star and the wind. He also mouths some of the most repugnant sentiments which Lawrence ever put on paper. Some of these are to do with race, some with the subjection of women to men, some with the need for great individuals to preside over the destiny of the masses. ' "I would like," Don Ramón says, "to be one of the Initiates of the Earth . . . forming a Natural Aristocracy of the World." ' Natural Aristocrats, he continues, ' "can be international, or cosmopolitan, or cosmic. It has always been so. The peoples are no more capable of it than the leaves of the mango tree are capable of attaching themselves to the pine." ' (pp. 260–261).

This spiritual pride in Ramón does not prevent him from having much of the aura and mystic interest which Rawdon Lilly fatally lacks in *Aaron's Rod*. Though *The Plumed Serpent* may seem faintly absurd to the modern reader, with its elaborate accounts of ritual worship verging on Biblical pastiche, it is more likely to be the form of the novel than the content which alienates people. Lawrence, through Ramón, speaks of the need for a regeneration of mystery in the world. ' "And a new Hermes should come back to the Mediterranean, and a new Ashtaroth to Tunis; and Mithras again to Persia, and Brahma unbroken to India, and the

Mexico: The pyramid at San Juan, Teotihuacan. *Mexican Government Tourist Department*

oldest of dragons to China." ' In other words, if each community in the world, led by the inspiration of great leaders, could resurrect what is true to its culture, temperament and climate, then no one religion would be more important than any other, yet all would be part of a global renewal of the spirit. Then, Ramón insists to Cipriano, 'I, First Man of Quetzalcoatl, with you, First Man of Huìtzilopochtli, and perhaps your Wife, First Woman of Itzpapolotl, could we not meet, with pure souls, the other great aristocrats of the world, the First Man of Wotan and the First Woman of Freya, First Lord of Hermes, and the Lady Astarte, the Best-Born of Brahma, and the son of the Greatest Dragon?' (p. 261). On the surface this may seem rhetorical and obscure, but it is no more than a plea for the coming-together of mankind in common resistance to the age of the machine and the tyranny of materialism. Many of the sub-cultures of the 1960's and 1970's have pleaded for the same ideal through not dissimilar means.

The Plumed Serpent must not be altogether exonerated from criticism, however. There is in the book a peculiar doctrine of blood separatism whereby the races of the world should remain pure from the corruption of inter-mingling. It also asserts more nakedly than in any other Lawrence novel the doctrine of male supremacy. When Kate marries Don Cipriano the ceremony enacts the sub-jection of woman to man, just as Teresa serenely accepts her servility to Ramón. The very landscape of Mexico, with its phallic cacti and 'sperm-like water' is evoked in terms of male sexuality. Ramón and Cipriano share an affinity of spirits which, in the episode where Cipriano is initiated into the role of the war-god, becomes explicitly physical. The general thesis of the novel argues for a positive will to revive our dormant spirituality, and thus it increasingly seems in tune with many people's attitudes today, but within this broad idea many of the particular doctrines in *The Plumed Serpent* remain peculiarly resistible. I suspect that Lawrence came to feel this for himself, for the novel loses some of its coherence towards the end. Kate, even in marriage, does not wholly commit herself either to Mexico or to Cipriano. Lawrence likewise becomes less convincing in his presentation of the revivalism as the novel moves to its close. Surely it is he who speaks through Kate in an italicized section on the last page. *What a fraud I am! I know all the time it is I who don't altogether want them. I want myself to myself. But I can fool them so that they shan't find out.*

The Plumed Serpent cannot be easily absorbed as an organic whole. Too many ideas proliferate, some almost contradicting others. There are long passages of ritual incantation. Yet the novel has a vigorous dramatic quality. Sometimes, as in the chapter entitled 'The attack on Jamil-tepec' or in the description of the bull-fight at the beginning, this arises from the same kind of powerful physical observa-tion which Lawrence so often displays in his travel-writings or in an essay such as 'Reflections on the Death of a Porcu-pine.' It comes, too, from the urgency of his concern for a new world. Though *The Plumed Serpent* is unlikely now to

Portrait in oils painted by Dorothy Brett in 1924.   *D. H. Lawrence Collection, University of Texas*

be read with wholehearted seriousness, it would be wrong to dismiss it as some kind of theatrical extravaganza. This is not the world of the Natcha-Kee-Tawaras but an earnest attempt to see what relevance a wholly different culture from our own may have to the kind of society we are still constructing.

11. *LADY CHATTERLEY'S LOVER*

To the proverbial man in the street *Lady Chatterley's Lover* probably still arouses the sniggers which surrounded it in 1960 when its publishers were taken to court on a charge of purveying obscenity. The novel made D. H. Lawrence a household name but for entirely the wrong reasons. He became identified with 'free love', 'permissiveness' and 'four-letter words', trends in the 1960s which might well have appalled the morally serious Lawrence. As a penalty for his new fame he became erroneously linked with sexual emancipation and frequently trivialized by people who did not understand his work. Even now it needs to be asserted that there are three central themes in *Lady Chatterley's Lover* which make nonsense of the myth that it offers a kind of intellectual's pornography. These themes are fidelity in human relationships, the erosion of old England, and the capacity of the English language to express more than conventional morality wishes it to say. Lawrence had touched on them all in earlier novels, but in *Aaron's Rod*, *Kangaroo* and *The Plumed Serpent* his intense concern with the possibilities of reforming society through different kinds of leadership had diverted him from any straightforward discussion of England, its mores, its society or its language. In his last novel (though he did not know it to be so), Lawrence wrote his most fully English work apart from *Sons and Lovers*. There are no Lydia Lenskys, Loerkes or Cicios here, no excursions abroad. Altogether abandoning the exotic territories of his previous three novels, Lawrence writes now of an England in which pastoralism and industrialization exist in uneasy conjunction.

There are three versions of *Lady Chatterley's Lover*. *The*

The Villa Mirenda, near Florence. In this olive grove, Lawrence wrote a large part of *Lady Chatterley's Lover*. *Photograph Gair Wilson*.

First Lady Chatterley, as William Heinemann Ltd. termed it when publishing it for the first time in England in 1972, is the shortest. Lawrence wrote it between October 1926 and March 1927. His next version, completed in the summer of 1927, is much longer. In its published form it is now known as *John Thomas and Lady Jane*. Both these earlier versions of *Lady Chatterley's Lover*, like the familiar third version, were first printed abroad, the first one appearing in America in 1944, the second in an Italian translation (by Carlo Izzo) in 1954. No version was legally available in Britain before 1960, when the uncut Florence edition of 1928 was re-published. This chequered writing and publishing history reflects the self-questioning attitude with which Lawrence approached his subject. He had always been an avid reviser of his own work but he clearly intended *Lady Chatterley's Lover* not only to be satisfactory in the form it took but to be explicit in its meaning. The three versions are thus cast in very different ways.

Frieda Lawrence, in her introduction to *The First Lady Chatterley*, expresses her preference for it because, she implies, it was the truest statement of what Lawrence wished to say: '*The First Lady Chatterley* he wrote as she came out of him, out of his own immediate self. In the third version he was also aware of his contemporaries' minds.' He kept adjusting the novel, Frieda tells us, because he was frightened that his critics would dismiss the book as mere mysticism (as *The Plumed Serpent* is still sometimes dismissed). He seems not to have bargained for the comparative indifference with which all three versions were treated for thirty years.

The First Lady Chatterley is the gentlest of the three, *John Thomas and Lady Jane* the most detailed, and *Lady Chatterley's Lover* the most polemical. Between the first and the second version Lawrence seems to have worried that the novel would be too dissociated from recognizable daily life. In the second, therefore, he emphasizes the effects of industrialization upon the beauties of England, he peoples the novel with more characters, and he balances pastoral lyricism with some degree of satire. The third version, the one most of us read first, is less changed from version two than version two is from its predecessor, even though it is only now that Lawrence's famous gamekeeper acquires the name Mellors (he is Parkin in the earlier versions). *Lady Chatterley's Lover* does, however, have a franker sexual vocabulary than either of the other versions. In a review in *The Times Literary Supplement* (27 April 1973) the anonymous writer maintains, at the end of an intelligently hostile assessment of the three works, that 'There is little point in offering an order of preference between the three versions. Certainly the first, comparatively free from jargon and overt bullying, is the least offensive: lacking the crudely opposed contrasts of *John Thomas and Lady Jane* and more especially of *Lady Chatterley's Lover*, it is more honest in observation, though correspondingly more obscure in purpose. But it does not make enough difference.'

The reviewer takes this point of view because he does not regard any version of *Lady Chatterley's Lover* as a major work of art, concluding, indeed, that 'much hatred lies within its assumption of tenderness'. I believe it does matter, however, which version we like best, for all three attempt different things. My own preference is for the familiar third version because it seems to possess a clarity of statement which, while it may be less 'honest' in the sense that it is less fair-minded than the previous drafts, overtly says what Lawrence primarily wanted to get across: namely that contemporary society in the western industrialized world is based on false values and that until we establish the right kind of relationships between individuals there can be no serious prospect of man fulfilling himself in anything but a mechanical way.

Lady Chatterley's Lover in its final form has the diagrammatic straightforwardness of a fable. Lady Chatterley, Mellors and Sir Clifford Chatterley have been pared down to prototypes, as though in an allegory. Lawrence had been moving towards this view of character in all his novels since *The Rainbow*, but in his final novel, in its final form, he has come to regard three-dimensional complexities of character as mere accretions. The novelist's task is to be spare, functional and explicit, as the earliest story-tellers were. *Lady Chatterley's Lover*, in this respect, looks forward to the formal experiments of modernism in fiction and back in time, as is appropriate in a novel eulogizing the English past, to the simple structure of primitive story-telling.

Of the three themes mentioned at the start of this discussion of *Lady Chatterley's Lover*, that of fidelity requires most explanation. Is not this a tale of marital infidelity? In a purely legal sense it is, but Lawrence creates in this novel a world so deeply private between Connie Chatterley and Oliver Mellors that it would be virtually sacrilegious to impose judicial restraints upon it. Clifford Chatterley embodies inherited privilege, atrophied power and sexual denial. He is socially boorish, insensitive to nature and physically impotent. He has no life in the novel (or in any version of it) other than as the symbolic manifestation of the mechanical will. To insist upon married fidelity between him and Connie would be to assert the superiority of social forms over instinctual behaviour. In the serious evaluation of right relationships Lawrence appropriately looks for trueness of feelings, not for conventions approved by a society he believed to be dying.

Connie's life as the lady of Wragby Hall is described early in the novel as 'void . . . spectral, not really existing' (p.19). When she gives herself sexually to Michaelis, a house-guest, it means nothing to her, only confirming the emptiness of her being. Lawrence describes the episode with reticence, in obvious contrast to the flowing rhythms with which he later writes of the lovemaking between Connie and Mellors. These early chapters magnificently define a world where talk is a substitute for action and where Chatterley can seriously intellectualize 'this sex thing' as a minor adjunct to 'the slow building up of integral personality' (pp. 46–47).

At the conclusion of this conversation we meet Mellors for the first time, 'like the sudden rush of a threat out of nowhere' (p. 48). He betokens a new kind of life, isolated from the social world but in obvious harmony with the natural environment, whose right balance it is his duty, as a gamekeeper, to ensure. Though their first encounters are wary, the relationship that develops between Connie and Mellors intensifies to a point where Clifford and his world become extraneous to the needs which the two lovers can fulfil in each other. At the end of the novel Connie is pregnant, awaiting her divorce and anticipating a future of true personal freedom.

In *The Times Literary Supplement* review already quoted this ending is reviled as escapism into a 'story-book future – for those who are lucky enough to be able to live the forest life. As for the rest, why, their future is none of our concern: they are simply the world which Connie will jettison for her own personal salvation.' The implied criticism of Lawrence's scheme has to be faced, and it is best to do so by remembering that though few individuals have the pastoral opportunities of Connie and Mellors, we all have the capacity to form relationships. In getting the private world right we may collectively come closer to a changed society. Having failed in *Kangaroo* and *The Plumed Serpent* to find a practical solution to the *malaise* in modern society, Lawrence approaches the problem from the other end, through private experience rather than public action.

The family of Chatterley 'stood for England and St. George', Lawrence tells us in the first chapter, and 'never knew there was a difference'. For Lawrence the true England is in the woods and valleys, not in the great houses. Ironically Sir Clifford also sees the woods as a symbol of England, even though his father had cut the trees to furnish the war effort – we think back to the crass leadership in the war which Lawrence indicts in *Kangaroo*. Clifford's woods, however, would always be private, untrespassed. They are 'property'. For Connie and Mellors they are the place where they make love, teeming with natural life and undestroyed beauty. Around them the spread of industrial England blots out more and more of the agricultural landscape. It is as though a black monster has been unleashed, feeding only on England's past.

It was as if dismalness had soaked through and through everything. The utter negation of natural beauty, the utter negation of the gladness of life, the utter absence of the instinct for shapely beauty which every bird and beast has, the utter death of the human intuitive faculty was appalling. (p. 158)

Lady Chatterley's Lover is a cry of lamentation for disappearing England. 'Ours is essentially a tragic age, so we refuse to take it tragically', Lawrence says in the opening line of the novel. The tragedy is that modern industrialized man has not been the innocent victim of malevolent gods, but has chosen this form of evolution. The only hope for him is that he will see how the process of destruction is not yet complete. The natural world has been contained but not destroyed. When Connie and Mellors place forget-me-nots in each other's sex-parts they express not only the tender intimacy of their love for each other, but their knowledge of a remembered England whose pattern of life was 'organic', not 'mechanical'. In a simple summary this sounds like nostalgic sentimentality, but the import of *Lady Chatterley's Lover* is severe, even brutal. Man must rescue himself or be blotted out. Lawrence hopes, surely, that we will see in Connie and Mellors the same archetypal representation of human possibilities that Milton intended in the expelled Adam and Eve.

Lawrence, in the third version of the Lady Chatterley story, writes an uncluttered prose which he steers into lyricism when he believes the theme requires it. He is in total command of his language now, with none of the poetic overwriting of his first novels, over-urgent didacticism of some passages in *The Rainbow* and *Women in Love*, or confused rhetoric occasionally detectable in the 'leadership' novels. *Lady Chatterley's Lover* does not have a single style, but finds at each stage an appropriate correspondence between language and subject. Since some of the novel describes sexual intercourse and explicit responses to sex, Lawrence needs to find an unequivocal language for this. The best sexual descriptions in the novel achieve a rhythm which conveys the sense of a wholly sensual experience. 'And it seemed she was like the sea, nothing but dark waves rising and heaving, heaving with a great swell, so that slowly her whole darkness was in motion, and she was ocean rolling its dark, dumb mass' (p. 181).

At moments such as this Lawrence is extending English prose in an attempt to realize virtually unrealizable sensations. Language can perhaps only be retrospective. When we burn ourselves we feel the pain, and only then do we articulate it. Sexual orgasm likewise lies beyond language, though almost every love poet has tried to recall it in a form of words that may capture the sense of the moment. Lawrence tries to realize the moment itself, to leave out the time-gap between experience and recollection. It leads him to adopt the kind of vocabulary which, sparsely used though it is, took the novel into the law courts. He rejoiced in his opportunity to release the English language from some of its prudery – none of the words which caused offence were less than several hundred years old – but he did not really find a way of making them seem less than quaint and archaic. Mellors is a fairly educated man, and his switches into regional speech where sexual words are supposed to sound natural smack too much of a literary device. Lawrence may not succeed, therefore, in realizing a new form of English capable of expressing non-linguistic sensations, but he was defeated more by the limitations of language itself than by his own approach to it.

Lady Chatterley's Lover was written by an ill man who could see almost nothing admirable in the way his society was moving. One might expect in the circumstances a cry of bitter despair, but the novel insists that the world is not only worth saving but that it can still be saved. Lawrence shows himself still interested in the power of the novel as an aesthetic form, experimenting almost dramatically with new methods of presenting character and using English. It is the final major work of fiction in his career, but it shows an artist still in full command of his gifts, capable of reviving some past strengths which more recent work had obscured, whilst at the same time inching his talents into new territory. D. H. Lawrence died in the midstream of his creative flow, not at the point where the river widens into the dark sea.

12. LAWRENCE'S OTHER FICTION

Though his ten novels must always be regarded as the basis of his claim to greatness as a writer, Lawrence was also the author of innumerable other works of fiction. Some critics have thought his shorter fiction better art than his full-length works because he necessarily denies himself the elaborations and diversions, the repetitions and the flights of metaphysical fancy which are integral to his novels. In a short account of these writings it is impossible to mention more than a few of the stories, novellas and other fictions unless this section is to degenerate into a mere list of titles, for they amount to well over seventy separate creations. None of them lacks interest; some of them are crucial to his development.

Not content to write novels of his own, Lawrence in 1923 spent a considerable amount of time re-working other people's fiction. The most famous outcome of this is *The Boy in the Bush* (1928), a revision of *The House of Ellis*, an unpublished novel by M. L. Skinner. He was honest with Mollie Skinner: 'You have no constructive power', he told her. He gave the novel (or so we must presume) the qualities which make it an engrossing if lightweight account of a young Australian's growth into manhood in the 1880s. 'The only thing was to write it all out again, following your MS almost exactly, but giving a unity, a rhythm, and a little more psychic development than you had done', he told the original author and she unresistingly accepted his amendments. At the same time Lawrence was translating a novel by the Sicilian writer Giovanni Verga, revising *Dragon of the Apocalypse* by Frederick Carter, and continuously reviewing fiction for various London journals.

In his correspondence Lawrence occasionally mentions a book that he is currently working on, which never finally saw the light of day or which was later published in another form. Almost every novel he wrote started with a different title. It would be an engaging quiz to ask who wrote, and by what other names are they known, the following novels: *Laetitia, The Saga of Siegmund, Paul Morel, The Sisters, The Bitter Cherry, Quetzalcoatl* and *Tenderness*, for only *Aaron's Rod* and *Kangaroo* seem to have survived under the titles Lawrence first mooted for them. One of the novels which never came to anything was to be about Robert Burns, a Lawrentian hero in embryo. It may have been a good thing that Lawrence never took the novel very far, because he intended to transplant the Scottish poet to a Derbyshire setting. A more determined attempt to write a novel which eventually came to nothing is *Mr. Noon*, a vivacious comedy which Lawrence started immediately after completing *The Lost Girl*.

Lawrence's first major story was 'The White Stocking' (1907), a prototype of the stories he was to write more maturely in later years, wherein a young wife is torn between decency towards her husband and her natural attraction to a man she meets at a dance. His first published tale was a slight piece entitled 'A Prelude', which he had submitted under Jessie Chambers' name for a literary competition in Nottingham. The first story to be printed under his own name was 'Goose Fair'.

Lawrence's rapid development as a writer can be seen if we compare these comparatively tenuous early stories with works like 'Odour of Chrysanthemums', a tale of grief in a mining community, and 'Daughters of the Vicar', in which he explores the social gulf which divides the English middle-class from the working-class. Only a few months separates all these works, but the intensity of Lawrence's writing has deepened immensely. They were published together in *The Prussian Officer, and other stories* (1914), which for many people remains his most satisfactory collection. The title story presents a relationship between an officer and his orderly as concentrated and sensual as any we encounter in the novels. It is tempting in a group of stories such as this to trace the links with other works, but each one has an individual power that bestows on it a separate existence. Though 'The Prussian Officer', for example, anticipates something of the Birkin-Crich relationship in *Women in Love*, it has its own kind of violent imagination. We reduce the stories if we see them only as antecedents of larger works.

The same must be said of the stories which appeared in the second collection published in his own lifetime, *England, My England, and other stories* (1922), of which at least three, the title story, 'The Horse Dealer's Daughter' and 'Fanny and Annie', are among the best he wrote. In 'England, my England' Lawrence means us to see Egbert, the main character, as a symbol of effete but not altogether impotent

English gentility. Lawrence possibly asks too much if he intends us to read the whole plight of this class into one short story, but in the final pages of this loosely-constructed tale he manages to conjure up for us the barbarity of war. By contrast 'The Horse Dealer's Daughter' creates a private world between a doctor and the girl he rescues from suicide. An intense but not altogether humourless climax brings the two of them to the point of marriage, as though their love has been fanned by the flames of the fire, before which they have been drying themselves. Within its own terms the story works well because Lawrence does not deviate from his tight control of atmosphere.

'Fanny and Annie' may serve as a representative example of Lawrence's short-story technique at this middle point in his writing career. It opens with characteristically Lawrentian vocabulary:

Flame-lurid his face as he turned among the throng of flame-lit and dark faces upon the platform. In the light of the furnace she caught sight of his drifting countenance, like a piece of floating fire.

A woman returns from a far place where she has been a lady's maid to be met by her first-love. The setting is industrial and the theme as much a conflict of attitudes within class as that between the Morels in *Sons and Lovers*, though Fanny does not have Mrs. Morel's different background. This is a coming home to claim her last opportunity to be a wife. She arrives 'with her umbrella, her chatelaine, and her little leather case', a mock lady with mock gentility. Harry, by contrast, 'had waited – or remained single – all these years', Lawrence carefully balancing irony and pathos. For that is the skill of this story. Fanny has to learn humility during the course of it and feels 'dragged down to earth, as a bird which some dog has got down in the dust', but the ending leaves it ambiguous as to whether Fanny's final assimilation into her old community is a resignation to the second-rate or a decent alternative to the non-life she has had as a maid. Lawrence is entirely fair to the Morley villagers in the tale, satirizing them lightly but never dismissively. It is a decent community, proud of its standards, its festivals, its cleanliness. Is not Fanny's return the moment of her release, not least sexually, for Harry has the gruff sexuality of Lawrence's natural man? However we interpret Fanny's history, this story displays Lawrence's technique at its sharpest. Image and theme constantly interrelate so that in only fifteen pages we have met a vivid group of people with the qualified hopes and unexpressed frustrations of countless numbers like them.

In 1923 'The Ladybird', 'The Fox' and 'The Captain's Doll' were published together. These three novellas were deeply admired by the most influential of Lawrence's critical advocates, F. R. Leavis. 'The inspiration, the *raison d'être*, of "The Captain's Doll" entails the convincing presentment of the Lawrentian themes in an action that shall affect us as belonging, not to a poetic-prophetic Sabbath world, as "The Ladybird" does, but to the everyday reality in which we live, though, unlike "The Fox", to a milieu of education and sophisticated people' (F. R. Leavis, *D. H. Lawrence: Novelist*, p. 212). Leavis admired 'The Captain's Doll' for its 'common sense', but many readers are more likely to be struck by its humour and by the way in which Lawrence appears to be parodying some of his own attitudes towards the relationship of the sexes. 'The Fox' is a study in tortured sexual relations, linking the human world with a symbolic value placed on animal behaviour. 'The Ladybird', in a much more stylized way, explores the kind of territory which *Lady Chatterley's Lover* successfully makes its own, contrasting sexless almost euphuistic love with true passion.

'St. Mawr' (1925) was described by Leavis as having 'a creative and technical originality more remarkable than that of *The Waste Land*, being, as that poem is not, completely achieved, a full and self-sufficient creation. It can hardly strike the admirer as anything but major' (*D. H. Lawrence: Novelist*, p. 235). 'St. Mawr' extends the symbolism of animals much further than the 'Rabbit' chapter in *Women in Love* or 'The Fox', for St. Mawr is a stallion resentful of the ignoble men who try to master him. The novella suffers from irrelevant Lawrentian diversions about 'the secret evil' in men which indulges their greed and death-wish, so that Leavis's judgement on it is now likely to seem overstressed for most readers, but it undoubtedly has a vigorous case to make against western civilization. Along with 'The Woman Who Rode Away' (1928), an unpleasant but brilliantly sustained tale of female submission to alien gods, it evokes a wholly foreign world which, repellent though it may be to many people, holds total conviction while we read of it.

Lawrence went on writing stories even in the less energetic final years of his life. They include 'The Virgin and the Gypsy' (1926, published 1930), which embodies almost definitively the theme of sexual attraction across class and even folk barriers, powerfully conveyed through an insinuatingly erotic use of imagery. 'Love Among the Haystacks' (though drafted much earlier) came out in 1930, 'The Man Who Died' (originally 'The Escaped Cock') and 'The Man Who Loved Islands', both 1929, and several pieces not published until after his death, show a writer constantly probing for new ways of expressing his concern for man's future and his fascination with human relationships. These late stories are sometimes too symbolically wrought to seem other than obsessional, but we seldom feel that Lawrence repeats himself. Even when the themes are familiar the imaginative form they take is usually unique.

Some critics claim that the short-story and the novella differ not just in length and scope but in their essential aesthetic being from the full-length novel. If this is so, then D. H. Lawrence proves the exception to the rule, for his shorter writings normally parallel themes and concepts in his novels. They are neither less nor more effective at their best, complete achievements in their own right which cast light on the novels only if that is how we want to use them. Though Lawrence maintained close contact with the main artist of the English short-story in the early part of the century, Katherine Mansfield, he never imitated her style. Nor did he borrow from the classic continental short-story writers. He found a voice so uniquely his own that one can open almost any page of one of his tales and recognize it as distinctively Lawrentian. Urgent prose, with carefully placed emphases and recurring key words; background detail fully creating the intended world yet corresponding to the emotional nature of the protagonists; private moods

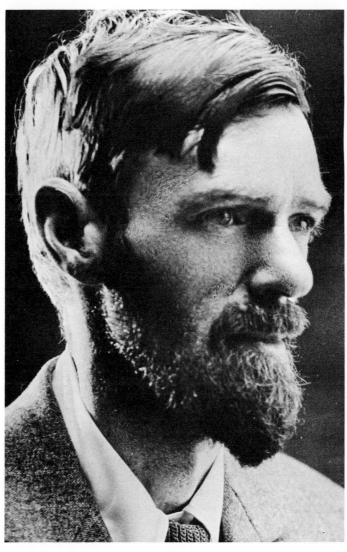

D. H. Lawrence in 1929. *British Council*

evoking public themes and metaphysics. It does not always work, but when it does, in a naturalistic tale such as 'Odour of Chrysanthemums' or in a ritualistic piece such as 'The Woman Who Rode Away', we see in Lawrence a complete master of the shorter narrative.

13. LAWRENCE AS A TRAVEL WRITER

Almost everything Lawrence wrote after *The White Peacock* reflects his personal odyssey. The early novels are full of excursions to English places such as the Isle of Wight (in *The Trespasser*), and Lincoln Cathedral (in *The Rainbow*). In *Women in Love, The Lost Girl* and *Aaron's Rod*, the novels of his middle period, Lawrence gives increasing emphasis to 'abroad'. In the early 1920s his correspondence becomes very bitter as he talks about England as a graveyard. There can be little doubt that he regarded the war as an historical disaster which totally failed to arrest the decline of moral wisdom he perceived throughout northern Europe. In 1928 he summed up his true feelings about England in the essay 'Dull London' – the hostility has gone and he expresses instead a profound distaste for the passionless nature of English society, as he saw it. The tone is regretful rather than aggressive.

Of course, England is the easiest country in the world, easy, easy and nice. Everbody is nice, and everybody is easy. The English people on the whole are surely the *nicest* people in the world, and everybody makes everything so easy for everybody else, that there is almost nothing to resist at all. But this very easiness and this very niceness become at last a nightmare. It is as if the whole air were impregnated with chloroform or some other pervasive anaesthetic, that makes everything easy and nice, and takes the edge off everything, whether nice or nasty. As you inhale the drug of easiness and niceness, your vitality begins to sink. Perhaps not your physical vitality, but something else: the vivid flame of your individual life. England can afford to be so free and individual because no individual flame of life is sharp and vivid. It is just mildly warm and safe. You couldn't burn your fingers at it. Nice, safe, easy: the whole ideal. And yet under all the easiness is a gnawing uneasiness, as in a drug-taker.

Apart from *Kangaroo* and *The Plumed Serpent*, Lawrence's main travel writings are three short books dating from the same period, *Sea and Sardinia* (1923), *Mornings in Mexico* (1927) and *Etruscan Places* (written 1927, published 1932). He wrote one earlier volume of travel pieces, *Twilight in Italy* (1916) in which there is much Christology and also some first-rate observation of Italian domesticity in which pagan associations are evoked. *Sea and Sardinia* is a more substantial attempt to render what Lawrence was constantly seeking, a society 'outside the circuit of civilization' (p. 9), which before he left Europe he instinctively felt would most probably be encountered in the remoter parts of Italy. 'The name of Athens hardly moves me', he writes in *Sea and Sardinia*, but on his journey to Sardinia from Palermo he begins to hear the 'terrible echo' which calls 'from the darkest recesses of my blood' (p. 40). Athens, the ancient seat of reason and learning, leaves him cold, but the territory in which he travels in *Sea and Sardinia*, real places rather than remembered notions, brings him into contact with unspoilt peasant communities where manly virtues still thrive. The Sardinian days are recalled with humour and vitality. There are almost no incursions into philosophical generalization. The result is a book which more straightforwardly places Lawrence as a Romantic writer than perhaps anything else he wrote, anti-rational, marrying instinct and intelligence.

This Sunday morning, seeing the frost among the tangled, still savage bushes of Sardinia, my soul thrilled again. This was not all known. This was not all worked out. Life was not only a process of rediscovering backwards. It is that, also; and it is that intensely. Italy has given me back I know not what of myself, but a very, very great deal. She has found for me so much that was lost: like a restored Osiris. But this morning in the omnibus I realize that, apart from the great rediscovery backwards, which one *must* make before one can be whole at all, there is a move forwards. There are unknown, unworked lands where the salt has not lost its savour. But one must have perfected oneself in the great past first. (p. 131)

Perfecting oneself in the great past is the author's dedicated intention in *Mornings in Mexico* and *Etruscan Places*. These sketches, though still in the episodically descriptive manner of the first two books, do not have the same kind of humanity. The interest is more abstract, more abstruse. The reader of *Sea and Sardinia* knows the ship's passengers, the bus drivers, the peasants, and the urchins whom we meet in Lawrence's vivid immediate style. He would today be in great demand as a travel commentator, implying social conclusions from anecdotal observations in the way that V. S. Naipaul and Paul Theroux now do in their travelogues, but it would be more for the manner of *Sea and Sardinia* than for the way he presents the later two books.

Mornings in Mexico ought to be read partly as a companion piece to *The Plumed Serpent*, though in some of the details of ancient rites it differs. The book comprises eight descriptions of Mexican or New Mexican life, the core of which are three essays on Didian dances. Dramatic and vigorous though these undoubtedly are, often discovering a prose rhythm to match the movement of the dance ('Mindless, without effort, under the hot sun, unceasing, yet never perspiring nor even breathing heavily, they dance on and on', p. 68), our principal interest in them today may be for the light they throw on the strange doctrines of Lawrence's Mexican novel. Here he defines his attraction to the animistic *credo* of the Aztec descendants, with their insistence on 'the mystic, living will that is in man' (p. 77). The Christian believes in a lost Paradise and a future Redemption, but in Lawrence's view he despises the present moment. Man feels himself unworthy of God. He is always, in the western tradition, exorcizing his original sin and seeking future grace, so that he has no immediate vitality. This, ultimately, explains the 'pervasive anaesthetic' he describes in 'Dull London' as a feature of English life: it derives not just from the northern temperament climatically, but from the religious sources in western man, with their insistence on past error, future need and present imperfectibility.

Etruscan Places, published posthumously, is incomplete, being six sketches towards an intended cycle of twelve. Lawrence visited the four sites he describes in the book in 1927. They are Cerveteri, Tarquinia, Vulci and Volterra.

Capo Malfatano, Sardinia: *Italian National Tourist Board*

Here he seeks knowledge of a civilization even more ancient and more 'lost' than that of the Aztecs, for the Etruscans have left nothing behind but paintings, tombs and the memorabilia of a people doomed to extinction through the colonizing power of brutal Rome (Lawrence's dislike of Roman classicism was as strong as his sentiments towards the Greeks). *Etruscan Places* is the work of an art critic rather than a novelist, though even here Lawrence's imagination constantly recreates the *personae* of Etruscan life. At this point of his life Lawrence turned to painting as his own main form of expression – his last ten years teem with pictures he made himself, pictures about which he wrote, and pictures he went long distances to see. In the heyday of the Etruscan civilization he finds evidence through their pictures of naturalness and feeling, though this is gradually eroded by rationality, scepticism and science, Roman qualities which deny 'red blood' and 'consciousness'.

In Lawrence's correspondence, which is now being edited in its entirety for the first time and published by the Cambridge University Press, proliferate comments and ideas about the places he visited from his first visits to Germany to his last days in France, supplements not only to his imaginative work but to his travel documentaries. Rootlessness and self-exile have become increasingly familiar among the writers of the twentieth-century, betokening the break-up of a shared assurance about permanent values in society. Lawrence is a major contributor to the literature of exile and though his travel writings do not especially add to our regard for him as a great writer, they undoubtedly make available details and evidence about him which considerably help our reading of his novels and poetry. In their own right they contain some of his finest prose moments, bringing to life alien landscapes and other cultures. 'I am English, and my Englishness is my very vision. But now I must go away, if my soul is sightless for ever, let it then be blind, rather than commit the vast wickedness of acquiescence', wrote Lawrence in a letter in October 1915. Through his travel writings we can perhaps find the clearest indication of how he avoided the blindness he feared might result from leaving the country of his birth.

Dance Sketch: Oil painting by D. H. Lawrence (1929). *Reproduced by kind permission of Laurence Pollinger Ltd. the Frieda Lawrence Estate and Saki Karavas.*

14. LAWRENCE THE POET

Lawrence's first published work were some poems selected on his behalf by Jessie Chambers and sent to the *English Review* where they appeared in November 1902.

> I have opened the window to warm my hands on the sill
> Where the sunlight soaks in the stone: the afternoon
> Is full of dreams, my love, the boys are all still
> In a wistful dream of Lorna Doone.

These opening lines from his first printed poem, 'Dreams Old and Nascent', are addressed to Jessie Chambers. If they do not announce the arrival of a great writer, they certainly indicate the young Lawrence's love of plain natural pleasures. Stillness and warmth, with the same mellowness as the pastoral chapters of *The White Peacock*, flood through the early part of the poem, but then 'The surface of dreams is broken' and the poet reaches almost in panic towards 'the terror of lifting the innermost I out of the sweep of the impulse of life'. We might detect some echoes of Hopkins and Yeats in the early Lawrence poems, but he is astonishingly free from other influences. Over-written and imprecise though he can occasionally be in his first poems, he nevertheless writes with the confidence that what he has to say matters.

Lawrence wrote poetry all his life. Eight collections were published in his own lifetime, *Love Poems and others* (1913), *Amores* (1916), *Look! We have come through!* (1917), *New Poems* (1918), *Boy* (1919), *Tortoises* (1921), *Birds, Beasts and Flowers* (1923) and *Pansies* (1929), in addition to the two volumes of his *Collected Poems*, which came out in 1928. Three more volumes were published posthumously, *Nettles* (1930), *Triumph of the Machine* (1930) and *The Ship of Death, and other poems* (1933). It amounts to an abiding concern for poetic expression, though just as one finds the word 'poetic' necessarily coming to mind when talking about so much of his prose, so it is impossible not to read some of his verse without feeling it is only rhetoric or metred prose. This reaction would not have dismayed Lawrence, who regarded divisions between literary genres as arbitrary and banal.

Lawrence's early poems, 1906–1911, are almost entirely autobiographical. Though their lyrical vocabulary is conventionally Georgian their tone and what he does with the words he chooses show a poet eager to express a personal vision. Describing a snap-dragon –

> Strangled, my heart swelled up so full
> As if it would burst its wine-skin in my throat,
> Choke me in my own crimson. I watched her pull
> The gorge of the gaping flower, till the blood did float
> Over my eyes, and I was blind.

or a water-hen –

> Oh, water-hen, beside the rushes
> Hide your quaint, unfading blushes,
> Still your quick tail, and lie as dead,
> Till the distance folds over his ominous tread.

– we see as explicitly as we do in any of the novels how attentive Lawrence was to the details of nature and how sympathetic to the struggle of small creatures before rampant man. Those extracts come from 'Snap-dragon' and 'Cruelty and Love', two of Lawrence's best first poems.

In *Look! We have come through!* Lawrence begins to experiment more drastically with form. Though many of the poems in this collection still rhyme and still retain the combination of ballad clarity and unaffected lyricism which characterizes the earlier work, others flow freely and meanderingly like spoken narratives.

> But why, before
> He waters the horses does he wash his heel?
> Jesus! – his spurs are red with shining blood!
> ('The Young Soldier with Bloody Spurs')

This dramatic semi-naturalistic quality becomes stronger in Lawrence's poetry. The poet's 'I' *persona* speaks up more frequently and the invocations to the life-forces in the universe are sounded as though in urgent conversation –

Come quickly, and vindicate us
against too much death.
Come quickly, and stir the rotten globe of the world from within,
burst it with germination, with world anew.

> ('Craving for Spring')

Lawrence's poems read well in poetry recitals because of this personalized vigour. Some poems, mainly in the *Birds, Beasts and Flowers* collection, are therefore standard anthology pieces.

> A snake came to my water-trough
> On a hot, hot day, and I in pyjamas for the heat,
> To drink there.

A poem beginning casually goes through a small moment of horror, 'a sort of protest against his withdrawing into that horrid black hole', before leaving the observer with 'something to expiate:/A pettiness' (from 'Snake'). The animal world can teach man much about the dignity of life or the naturalness of behaviour in an unscientific mentality. Always Lawrence admires unconscious instinctive being in the creatures he observes. 'Fish, oh Fish/So little matters!' ('Fish'); 'She watches with insatiable wistfulness./Untold centuries of watching for something to come.' ('Kangaroo'); 'Such silence, such suspended transport.' ('Mosquito'). These creature-poems are told with humour, for Lawrence sees the comedy in his attempts to outwit an insect, a bat or a wolf, but beneath them all lies a vast admiration of forms of life which float freely in the world without responsibility or ambition. Lawrence does not sentimentalize his subjects – as his title-essay in *Reflections on the Death of a Porcupine* indicates, he understood the predatory instincts in all living things (even in plants he might have added), but he achieves in *Birds, Beasts and Flowers* his twin aim of making observed nature dramatic and symbolic. Each subject lives in his poems individually, but each manifests the dark powers of the universe with which he constantly seeks to make contact.

As one would expect, the poetry which Lawrence wrote in the 1920s (though between 1923 and 1928 he wrote very little) matches the grand exploratory themes of his novels in the same period. It is summed up in 'Terra Incognita' –

There are vast realms of consciousness still undreamed of
vast ranges of experience, like the humming of unseen harps,
we know nothing of, within us.
O when man has escaped from the barbed-wire entanglement
of his own ideas and his own mechanical devices
there is a marvellous rich world of contact and sheer fluid beauty
and fearless face-to-face awareness of now-naked life.

Urgent free-flowing verse of this kind can hardly escape an accusation of repetitiousness, even of boring the reader, but at its best (in 'Thought' or in 'Bavarian Gentians') Lawrence disciplines his language so that his prophetic desperation about mankind carries conviction. His last poems are so strongly shadowed by the possibility of death that even when they lose much poetic concentration in terms of form they still exert a powerful emotional force. 'But still I know that life is for delight' he says in 'Kissing and Horrid Strife'. Here, as in his poems of triumph over death, 'The Ship of Death' and 'Shadows', he discovers a gravity of diction and calmness of utterance which are deeply affecting. All rhetoric is gone now and only his strict need to go on insisting that life is worth fighting for in a dying world – the world's death, not his own – keeps him from silence.

> then I must know that still
> I am in the hands of the unknown God,
> he is breaking me down to his own oblivion
> to send me forth on a new morning, a new man.
>
> ('Shadows')

The last poems of Lawrence have this religious sobriety because the mood is intense and the language unstrained. He was a poet capable of greatness only in a few animal poems and in these last pieces on mortality, but in everything he wrote for his poetry collections he expressed himself as though this poem in hand was all that really mattered. We never feel that he is being a dilettante or that his verses are idle compositions on a rest day. They vary wildly in quality but they can never be said to lack conviction or to be less than full of passionate intensity.

15. LAWRENCE IN THE THEATRE

Like Henry James, Lawrence was a great novelist who hankered for recognition in the theatre but failed even remotely to attain it in his own lifetime. Unlike James, whose work remains largely untouched in the standard repertoire today, Lawrence has since the mid-1960s undergone considerable re-estimation as a dramatist, and at least one of his plays, *The Daughter-in-Law* (1913), is now regularly performed in British provincial playhouses. He wrote eight plays in all, though only three of them were published in his own lifetime, *The Widowing of Mrs. Holroyd* (1914), *Touch and Go* (1920) and *David* (1926). They span all his writing career, probably starting with *A Collier's Friday Night* ('written when I was twenty-one, almost before I'd done anything, it is most horribly green') and concluding with his Biblical epic *David* at the point in his career when he was most obsessed with old religions. His other plays are *The Merry-go-Round* (probably 1910), *The Married Man* (1912) and *The Fight for Barbara* (also 1912). He also, when in New Mexico in 1924 and 1925, began two other plays, tentatively called *Altitude* and *Noah's Flood*, though these are hardly more than fragments.

The theatre plays quite a central part in Lawrence's fiction. In *The White Peacock* he writes of George and Meg 'shaken with a tumult of wild feeling' at a performance of *Carmen*, as though the combination of music and drama has brought them into contact with a special kind of life: 'their eyes were blinded by a spray of tears and that strange quivering laughter which burns with real pain' (p. 286). Siegmund in *The Trespasser* and Aaron in *Aaron's Rod* play in theatre orchestras. The Natcha-Kee-Tawara troupe is the catalyst in *The Lost Girl*. Many of the rituals in *The Plumed Serpent* are presented dramatically, with an emphasis on formal speech and patterned action. Lawrence wrote about the theatre in *Twilight in Italy* and about dance in *Mornings in Mexico*. He is also known to have taken a practical interest in stage production when teaching at Croydon, was concerned to have the respect of the leading playwright of the day, Bernard Shaw ('one of those delightful people who give one the exquisite pleasure of falling out with him wholesomely', he wrote in 1908), and made efforts, normally without success, to see his own plays staged. On the other hand, he wrote almost nothing on contemporary European theatre, even though his lifetime saw the introduction of a regional repertory movement, the rise of German expressionism, the main impact of Ibsen and Chekhov after their

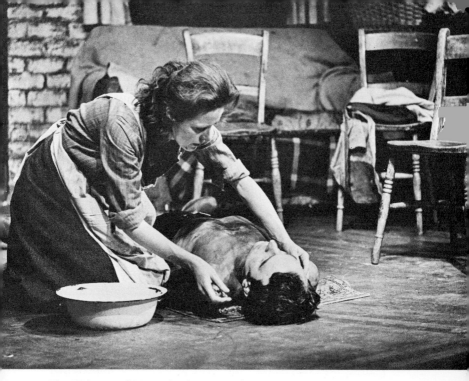

The Widowing of Mrs Holroyd. A scene from the Royal Court Theatre production directed by Peter Gill in 1968. *Douglas H. Jeffery*

deaths, and a revolution in ways of producing Shakespeare which endorsed precisely those qualities of natural feeling and unmannered simplicity that Lawrence sought for in his own work.

Lawrence's plays were ignored for so long that it has become customary to think of them as diversions, scripts he wrote because he was a compulsive writer taking time off from his more serious work in the novels and essays. Recent productions, however, have suggested a real dramatic ability in these works. They act well and are therefore likely to be seen more frequently. The process by which they have become accepted in the theatre has been extraordinarily slow. In his lifetime only two were staged, *The Widowing of Mrs. Holroyd*, initially in an amateur performance and eventually, in 1926, professionally, and *David*, in a production by the Stage Society. An adaptation of *The Daughter-in-Law* by Walter Greenwood, entitled *My Son's*

My Son, was given in London in 1936, but the unadulterated play itself had to wait until 1967 when Peter Gill, a young director who has himself developed into a sensitive playwright, staged it at the Royal Court Theatre.

There followed in 1968 a D. H. Lawrence season at the Royal Court when Gill revived *The Daughter-in-Law* alongside *A Collier's Friday Night* (which he had staged without décor for a single performance at the same theatre in 1965) and *The Widowing of Mrs. Holroyd* (televised in 1961 but unstaged since 1926). This brilliantly successful season radically altered the standard view of Lawrence as lumpily unstageable. It became apparent that the British theatre had an important dramatist of working-class attitudes writing at a time when the *bourgeois* taste of almost every playgoer prevented his work being performed. We know that Harley Granville Barker had politely declined to stage *The Widowing of Mrs. Holroyd* in 1911, three years before its publication, at a time when he was attempting (ironically also at the Royal Court) to inject more social realism into the English theatre, but it is very strange that between then and the 1960s there was such a total dearth of response to Lawrence's plays.

Lawrence's other plays have not been widely performed. Gill staged *The Merry-go-Round* at the Royal Court in 1973. It is a sleeker play than the earlier trio which he had directed and on this occasion he 'doctored' the text substantially. A production of *The Fight for Barbara* was presented at London's Mermaid Theatre in 1967 as part of a Lawrence evening, but the non-naturalistic elements in this rather stylized play surprised the critics who received it badly. The Oxford Playhouse staged a first production of *Touch and Go* in 1979. *The Married Man* has not received a recorded performance; nor have the two unfinished pieces. *David*, too, would seem to demand another opportunity to be seen on the stage since Robert Atkins's production in 1927 was mounted without the necessary resources, and at a time when critics and public were less inclined to take Lawrence's religiosity seriously.

Though the priority at the moment must be to see Lawrence's plays given a chance to establish themselves in the theatrical repertoire, it is already impossible to see or read them without relating them to the novels being written at the same time. Indeed, Lawrence perhaps used his plays as a chance to work out some of the issues and characters with which he was struggling simultaneously in his fiction. The most obvious example of this is *Touch and Go*, a play about the relationship between workers and managers which he created whilst writing *Women in Love*. Though the social debate in this play forms its core, the Lawrentian desire to see 'a new freedom, a new life' enshrined in each individual gives it a metaphysical element too. The main male character in *Touch and Go*, Gerald Barlow, sympathetically extends our understanding of men like Gerald Crich.

Lawrence's lasting reputation as a dramatist will probably rest on the three first plays he wrote, for in these he captures the spirit of industrialized living without resorting to sentimentality. In *The Daughter-in-Law* especially the clash between two generations of women for the possession of Luther Gascoigne is realized through a vigorous use of dialect. The themes of this play, *A Collier's Friday Night* and *The Widowing of Mrs. Holroyd*, echo elements in *Sons and Lovers*, but the dramatic presentation has a muscularity of its own, for in each case Lawrence eschews the poeticizing language and semi-mystic elaborations which suit passages in his fiction but which would seem theatrically stilted. Indeed, *The Fight for Barbara* and *The Married Man* are unlikely to gain the same kind of place in the theatre because they are more artificial and theoretical. *David*, being the story of David, Saul and Jonathan, makes no attempt at naturalism and might have a hieratic credibility if given a careful production. More probably, though, it will remain principally known on the page, an adjunct to the leadership novels. It is another study in male friendship and the possibilities of autocracy.

If one has a preconception that novelists and poets stray into drama only to the embarrassment of their reputations then D. H. Lawrence proves one wrong. He will almost certainly not now be neglected on the stage as he was for forty years. The case for his drama must not be overstated, however. He always wrote lively argumentative dialogue in his fiction and he gave careful consideration to the structure of each plot he devised, but though these are dramatic strengths they do not by themselves make for a great playwright. Lawrence's plays lack the tight unfolding of the best naturalistic drama. They flare into life with marvellous intensity on some occasions – *The Daughter-in-Law*, Act II, Scene iv, for example, where Minnie and Mrs. Gascoigne talk about their menfolk, or *David*, Scene ii, where Samuel prays for Saul – but the effects are intermittent. 'The actual technique of the stage is foreign to me', Lawrence said in 1927 when writing to a possible producer of *David*.

He was partly right, but we ought to remember that the two kinds of play he handled best, working-class naturalism and stylized religious pastiche, have never been greatly popular in the theatre. Though the former has been in vogue for some years now it may be that Lawrence's regionalism will vitiate his impact, for the Nottinghamshire dialect of the early plays is difficult to reproduce credibly. As for Lawrence's Biblical play *David* it requires an epic form of presentation which will always mean it is rarely performed even in the unlikely event of a return to favour of this kind of drama. *David* is Lawrence's most ambitious play and in some ways the one he cared about most – he even wrote the music for its original production. His durability in the theatre will centre, however, on *The Daughter-in-Law* and perhaps on *The Widowing of Mrs. Holroyd*. They will be performed partly out of curiosity value, minor works of a great novelist, but in their own right they would eventually have achieved some kind of status, even if their author had written nothing else.

16. LAWRENCE'S ESSAYS AND CORRESPONDENCE

'Essays' is a poor word for these brilliantly-varied writings, since 'an essay' unhappily implies something formal and academic and highbrow, whereas Lawrence was always intensely personal and spontaneous, with such a horror of pedantry and the university manner that he vastly preferred to be slangy and jaunty. 'Non-fictional prose' is worse than 'essay', so until somebody coins a better word we must stick to essays, though in Lawrence's case the word is more like a reference number than a description of literary form.

So writes Richard Aldington in his Introduction to the Penguin edition of Lawrence's *Selected Essays*. But the word 'essay' derives from the French 'essayer', to try, and in this sense completely justifies its use for D. H. Lawrence. His essays are attempts at definition, struggles to articulate complex attitudes to society, literature, sex, religion, education and philosophy. In almost every one the academic pen can score out paragraphs as redundant because the point has already been adequately made, but to do this is to bring ruination to a style that relies on underlining and insistence. Against the change that he is dogmatic, preachy or rhetorical Lawrence could validly reply, 'Who listens to me?'. He forces home his points for fear of being ignored. He is ignored less because of the manner in which he speaks – though few of his champions would want to maintain that his essays demonstrate his best prose – than because what he has to say so often seems unpalatable.

Many of Lawrence's essays disappeared from sight during his own lifetime, buried in obscure journals or remaining unpublished. Now, however, virtually everything is in print. Not all of it requires apology or explanation. Essays like 'Nottingham and the Mining Country' and 'Dull London' to which I have referred in accounts of his imaginative work, are hardly likely to evoke controversy; even though the point of view is distinctively Lawrentian, essays of this kind obviously record a personal response to remembered experience and it would be as inappropriate to challenge them as to say that Andrew Marvell had no right to speak thus to his coy mistress or that Keats is wrong to insist that a thing of beauty is a joy forever.

Two of Lawrence's longer treatises. *Psychoanalysis and the Unconscious* (1921), and its continuation *Fantasia of the Unconscious* (1922), argue the case for harmony between man and his environment. In them he denounces 'the mechanical principle' which he saw prevailing in modern society and which he felt to vitiate many of the procedures of Freudian psychoanalysis. These works are best read now as illuminating adjuncts to his novels, particularly to *The Rainbow* and *Women in Love*.

Lawrence is on more vulnerable ground with his literary criticism. His 'Study of Thomas Hardy' (1914), for example, contains a number of factual inaccuracies about Hardy's work as well as some silly dismissive statements. On form, however, Lawrence can be crisply perceptive, as he is here when pointing out Hardy's main greatness –

His feeling, his instinct, his sensuous understanding is, however, apart from his metaphysic, very great and deep, deeper than that, perhaps of any other English novelist. Putting aside his metaphysic, which must always obtrude when he thinks of people, and turning to the earth, to landscape, then he is true to himself.

Lawrence felt impassioned about literature, particularly about the novel. He did not care if a writer lacked the limited particularity of an Arnold Bennett providing he was 'man alive', that is, fully responsive to the currents which provide life to the body and significance to the universe. When he insists on 'blood consciousness' in so many of his works he is basically seeking for a metaphor to express this sense of currency, or flow, within living things. 'Let us learn from the novel', he says in 'Why the Novel Matters' – the same essay in which he talks of 'man alive'. 'In the novel, the characters can do nothing but *live*. If they keep on being good, according to pattern, or bad, according to pattern, or even volatile, according to pattern, they cease to live, and the novel falls dead.' This is his charge against Galsworthy, Bennett, even, obscurely, against Dostoievsky. 'A character in a novel has got to live, or it is nothing. We, likewise, in life have got to live, or we are nothing.' Hence Lawrence's verdict on Conrad ('I can't forgive Conrad . . . for giving in'), on Forster ('Life is more interesting in its undercurrents than in its obvious; and E. M. does see people, people and nothing but people: *ad nauseam*'), on Joyce ('utterly without spontaneity or real life'). I glean these last remarks from letters he wrote, for it is often in his correspondence that a chance observation crystallizes something which pages of overstatement in the essays have blurred.

Lawrence wrote several letters a day almost all his life. As the majority of these went to fellow writers, or to publishers, or to editors, they obviously document a living dialogue between him and the *literati* of his day. He was personally friendly with Aldous Huxley, H. G. Wells, Compton Mackenzie and Katherine Mansfield, and even when strains came into the relationships he would write an honest view of their work.

Some of Lawrence's literary subjects deviate wildly from the topic apparently planned. His essay on 'Pornography and Obscenity,' for example, lampoons *Jane Eyre* as 'much nearer to pornography than is Boccaccio' only a couple of pages before it goes on excessively about masturbation as 'certainly the most dangerous sexual vice that a society can be afflicted with'. Juxtaposition of ideas in this way can only work if there is a tight controlling argument, but Lawrence is thinking with his heart, battering us with unsubstantiated generalizations. Within the framework of a novel, even one as extravagantly ritualized as *The Plumed Serpent*, such a technique may carry weight. It fails to do so in many of the essays. It fails partly because Lawrence forgets at these times his central belief that nothing in life should be stationary or fixed, that the flow must always proceed, nothing be totally defined because even the word, liberator of expression though it is, can also be a gaoler. As he says of reading books, 'once it is *known*, and its meaning is fixed or established, it is dead'.

This last statement comes from *Apocalypse* (1931, p. 4). This was Lawrence's final major work, completed a few weeks before he died. Beginning as an introduction to a book by Frederick Carter, it developed into a free-flowing commentary on the Book of Revelation, imagery from which he had used in *The Rainbow* and to which he now returned in the passionate conviction that beneath what he understood to be a mainly allegorical structure the last book of the Bible held part of the key to an interpretation of life. Some of *Apocalypse* is almost incoherent, some of it pretentiously numerological, but the kernel carries on from where *The Plumed Serpent* drifted unconvincingly to a close. 'All religion, instead of being religion of *life*, here and now, became religion of postponed destiny' (p. 37), he writes. In his last and longest essay he once again appeals for a regenerated religion which will inform the life in hand and not the possibly mythical life to come.

Many of Lawrence's essays will strike the reader as idiosyncratic; some of his prolific correspondence is quirky or ill-tempered. Surely, however, we are fortunate to have this extra body of material to throw sudden illumination on the major texts, or simply to enlarge our knowledge of Lawrence's place in the contemporary literary world. A work of art is entire in its own right and I am not suggesting that *Sons and Lovers* cannot be read independently of 'Nottingham and the Mining Country', or that *The Plumed Serpent* will be any the less obscure because one has encountered *Apocalypse*. Even *Lady Chatterley's Lover* does not need the essay 'A Propos of *Lady Chatterley's Lover*' which Lawrence wrote as an explanation of the novel's 'phallic reality'. He meant these essays to be read, however, by anyone who wanted to follow his chain of thought. Sometimes they are too strident to be helpful, but on balance they clarify far more than they cloud. As for his letters, now being edited in complete form for the first time, we find in them a record of a major novelist reacting to the world as he experienced it day by day. Often they have a beauty of language as controlled as famous passages in the novels, but these come to us as sudden moments of wonder. Almost alone among his writings Lawrence wrote letters without ever intending to revise them. Here, very often, we detect the immediate Lawrence, the man of spontaneous feeling who has not fretted for the right phrase or channelled the observation into a distorting theoretical mould. In his letters we can approach the real man, and in the essays we often find the artist with his defences down. Both are indispensable.

17. CRITICS ON D. H. LAWRENCE: A NOTE

Lawrence wrote so trenchantly about other writers and about the art of fiction that it can only be with the greatest trepidation that anyone writes about his work. After his

The Lawrence Memorial Chapel above Taos, New Mexico. Lawrence's ashes are kept in the chapel: Frieda Lawrence's grave is outside. *Warren Roberts and Laurence Pollinger Ltd.*

death a number of generally critical reminiscences about him were published by people he liked to consider his friends. The fairest and most pertinent of these is *The Savage Pilgrimage* (1932) by Catherine Carswell. F. R. Leavis pioneered the academic study of Lawrence's work, eventually placing him in a line of great novelists descending from Jane Austen. Leavis's interest in Lawrence was primarily moral. For all its convoluted prose and occasionally weird judgements Leavis's *D. H. Lawrence: Novelist* (1955) remains essential reading. *Thoughts, Words and Creativity* (1976) elaborates upon, but does not greatly add to, the emphases of the earlier book, but it shows how even in old age Leavis regarded Lawrence as the consummate twentieth-century English writer. In recent years there have been many accounts of Lawrence's writing, including 'casebook' studies of individual texts. Among the best of the general studies are Keith Sagar's *The Art of D. H. Lawrence* (1966), Frank Kermode's *Lawrence* (1973), an intelligently provocative Freudian *critique*, and F. B. Pinion's *A D. H. Lawrence Companion* (1978). Emile Delavenay's *D. H. Lawrence: The Man and His Work* (revised 1972) and Harry T. Moore's *The Priest of Love* (revised 1974) are the best biographies, with Martin Green's *The Von Richthofen Sisters* (1974) a useful adjunct. I have personally found Sagar's *D. H. Lawrence: A Calendar of His Works* (1979) as invaluable a contribution to the study of a great writer as any produced in recent years. It documents on a day-to-day basis the course of Lawrence's writing, publication schedules and travels, authenticating evidence that was previously only supposition and discrediting some long established falsehoods.

D. H. LAWRENCE
A Select Bibliography
(Place of publication London, unless stated otherwise)
A definitive edition of Lawrence's works is being published by the Cambridge University Press.

Bibliographies

A BIBLIOGRAPHY OF THE WRITINGS OF D. H. LAWRENCE, by E. D. McDonald; Philadelphia (1925).

A BIBLIOGRAPHICAL SUPPLEMENT, by E. D. McDonald; Philadelphia (1931).

THE MANUSCRIPTS OF D. H. LAWRENCE, by L. C. Powell; Los Angeles (1937).

THE FRIEDA LAWRENCE COLLECTION OF D. H. LAWRENCE MANUSCRIPTS, by E. W. Tedlock; Albuquerque (1948).

D. H. LAWRENCE: A Checklist, by William Whyte; Detroit (1950).

'Criticism of D. H. Lawrence: A Selected checklist with an index to studies of separate works', by M. Beebe and A. Tommasi, *Modern Fiction Studies*, 5, 1, Spring 1959, 83–98.

A BIBLIOGRAPHY OF D. H. LAWRENCE, by Warren Roberts (1963)
—the standard bibliography. Includes details of periodical publications.

THE ART OF D. H. LAWRENCE, by Keith Sagar; Cambridge (1966)
—contains a useful 'Chronology' at the head of each chapter. Includes information on periodical publications.

Collections

THE PHOENIX EDITION (1935–   )
THE PENGUIN EDITION (1948–   )
—a more reliable edition.

PHOENIX: The Posthumous Papers of D. H. Lawrence, edited with an Introduction by E. D. McDonald (1936)
—contains the 'Study of Thomas Hardy', 'The Reality of Peace', 'Introduction to these Paintings', 'Democracy', 'Education of the People', 'John Galsworthy', and many essays, reviews and introductions.

PHOENIX II: Uncollected, unpublished and other prose works by D. H. Lawrence, collected and edited with an Introduction and notes by Warren Roberts and H. T. Moore (1968)
—includes 'The Crown'.

COMPLETE POEMS, 2 vols (1964).

COMPLETE PLAYS (1965).

Note: A complete edition of Lawrence's works, including letters, is being undertaken by Cambridge University Press.

Letters

THE LETTERS OF D. H. LAWRENCE, ed. Aldous Huxley (1932).

D. H. LAWRENCE'S LETTERS TO BERTRAND RUSSELL, ed. H. T. Moore; New York (1948).

THE COLLECTED LETTERS OF D. H. LAWRENCE, ed. H. T. Moore, 2 vols; New York (1962).

LAWRENCE IN LOVE: Letters from D. H. L. to Louie Burrows, ed. J. T. Boulton; Nottingham (1968).

LETTERS FROM D. H. LAWRENCE TO MARTIN SECKER, 1911–1930 (1970).

THE QUEST FOR RANANIM: D. H. Lawrence's letters to Koteliansky, 1914–1930, ed. G. J. Zytaruk; Montreal [1970].

D. H. LAWRENCE: Letters to Thomas and Adèle Seltzer, ed. G. M. Lacy; Santa Barbara (1976).

The Cambridge University Press is undertaking a fuller edition of Lawrence's letters.

Separate Works

THE WHITE PEACOCK (1911). *Novel*

THE TRESPASSER (1912). *Novel*

LOVE POEMS AND OTHERS (1913).

SONS AND LOVERS (1913). *Novel*

THE WIDOWING OF MRS. HOLROYD: A Drama in three acts; New York (1914).

THE PRUSSIAN OFFICER, AND OTHER STORIES (1914)
—contains 'The Prussian Officer', 'The Thorn in the Flesh', 'Daughters of the Vicar', 'A Fragment of Stained Glass', 'The Shades of Spring', 'The Soiled Rose', 'Second Best', 'The Shadow in the Rose Garden', 'Goose Fair', 'The White Stocking', 'A Sick Collier', 'The Christening', 'Odour of Chrysanthemums'.

THE RAINBOW (1915). *Novel*

TWILIGHT IN ITALY (1916). *Travel sketches*

AMORES: Poems (1916).

LOOK! WE HAVE COME THROUGH! (1917). *Verse*

NEW POEMS (1918).

BAY: A Book of Poems (1919).

TOUCH AND GO: A Play in Three Acts (1920).

WOMEN IN LOVE; New York (1920). *Novel*
—the first English edition was published in 1921.

THE LOST GIRL (1920). *Novel*

MOVEMENTS IN EUROPEAN HISTORY, by Lawrence H. Davison [*pseud.*] (1921). *Essays.*

PSYCHOANALYSIS AND THE UNCONSCIOUS; New York (1921). *Essay*

TORTOISES; New York (1921). *Verse*

SEA AND SARDINIA; New York (1921). *Travel*

AARON'S ROD; New York (1922). *Novel*

FANTASIA OF THE UNCONSCIOUS; New York (1922). *Essay*

ENGLAND, MY ENGLAND, AND OTHER STORIES; New York (1922)
—contains 'England, my England', 'Tickets Please', 'The Blind Man',
'Monkey Nuts', 'Wintry Peacock', 'You Touched Me', 'Samson
and Delilah', 'The Primrose Path', 'The Horse Dealer's Daughter',
'Fanny and Annie'.

THE LADYBIRD: 'The Ladybird', 'The Fox', 'The Captain's Doll' (1923).
Stories

STUDIES IN CLASSIC AMERICAN LITERATURE; New York (1923). *Criticism.*

KANGAROO (1923). *Novel*

BIRDS, BEASTS AND FLOWERS: Poems (1923).

THE BOY IN THE BUSH (1924). *Novel*
—with M. L. Skinner.

ST MAWR: Together with 'The Princess' (1925). *Stories*

REFLECTIONS ON THE DEATH OF A PORCUPINE, AND OTHER ESSAYS;
Philadelphia (1925).

THE PLUMED SERPENT: Quetzalcoatl (1926). *Novel*

DAVID: A Play (1926).

SUN (1926). *Story*

GLAD GHOSTS (1926). *Story*

MORNINGS IN MEXICO (1927). *Travel sketches*

RAWDON'S ROOF: A Story (1928).

THE WOMAN WHO RODE AWAY, AND OTHER STORIES (1928)
—contains 'Two Blue Birds', 'Sun', 'The Woman Who Rode Away',
'Smile', 'The Border Line', 'Jimmy and the Desperate Woman',
'The Last Laugh', 'In Love', 'Glad Ghosts', 'None of That'.

LADY CHATTERLEY'S LOVER; Florence (1928). *Novel*

THE COLLECTED POEMS OF D. H. LAWRENCE: Vol. I, Rhyming Poems
(1928), Vol. II, Unrhyming Poems (1928).

SEX LOCKED OUT (1929). *Essay*

THE PAINTINGS OF D. H. LAWRENCE (1929).

PANSIES: Poems (1929).

MY SKIRMISH WITH JOLLY ROGER; New York (1929). *Essay*

A PROPOS OF LADY CHATTERLEY'S LOVER: being an essay extended from
My Skirmish with Jolly Roger (1930).

PORNOGRAPHY AND OBSCENITY (1929). *Essay*

THE ESCAPED COCK; Paris (1929). *Story*

NETTLES (1930). *Verse*

ASSORTED ARTICLES (1930).

THE VIRGIN AND THE GIPSY; Florence (1930). *Story*

LOVE AMONG THE HAYSTACKS, AND OTHER PIECES (1930). *Stories and
sketches*

—contains 'Love Among the Haystacks', 'A Chapel Among the Mountains', 'A Hay Hut Among the Mountains', 'Once'.

TRIUMPH OF THE MACHINE (1930 [1931]). *Verse*

THE MAN WHO DIED (1931)
—extended version of *The Escaped Cock*.

APOCALYPSE: Florence (1931). *Essay*

A LETTER FROM CORNWALL (1931).

ETRUSCAN PLACES (1932). *Sketches*

LAST POEMS; Florence (1932).

THE LOVELY LADY (1933). *Stories*
—contains 'The Lovely Lady', 'Rawdon's Roof', 'The Rocking-Horse Winner', 'Mother and Daughter', 'The Blue Moccasins', 'Things', 'The Overtone', 'The Man Who Loved Islands'.

WE NEED ONE ANOTHER; New York (1933). *Essays*

THE SHIP OF DEATH, AND OTHER POEMS (1933).

A COLLIER'S FRIDAY NIGHT (1934). *Play*

A MODERN LOVER (1934)
—contains 'A Modern Lover', 'The Old Adam', 'Her Turn', 'Strike Pay', 'The Witch à la Mode', 'New Eve and Old Adam', 'Mr Noon'.

FOREWORD TO 'WOMEN IN LOVE'; San Francisco (1936)
—not originally published with the novel; first included with Random House Modern Library edition.

FIRE AND OTHER POEMS; San Francisco (1940).

THE FIRST LADY CHATTERLEY; New York (1944)
—the first version of *Lady Chatterley's Lover*.

THE SYMBOLIC MEANING: The uncollected versions of *Studies in Classic American Literature*; ed. Armin Arnold (1962).

JOHN THOMAS AND LADY JANE: the second version of *Lady Chatterley's Lover* (1972).

THE LETTERS OF D. H. LAWRENCE: Vol. I (1901–13), ed. by James T. Boulton; Cambridge (1979).

Works Translated by D. H. Lawrence

ALL THINGS ARE POSSIBLE, by Leo Shestov. Authorized translation by S. S. Koteliansky. With a foreword by D. H. Lawrence (1920)
—Lawrence is known to have collaborated in the translation.

THE GENTLEMAN FROM SAN FRANCISCO, AND OTHER STORIES, by I. A. Bunin. Translated from the Russian by S. S. Koteliansky and L. Woolf (1922)
—Lawrence was co-translator of the title story.

MASTRO-DON GESUALDO, by Giovanni Verga, translated by D. H. Lawrence; New York (1923).

LITTLE NOVELS OF SICILY, by Giovanni Verga, translated by D. H. Lawrence; New York (1925).

CAVALLERIA RUSTICANA, AND OTHER STORIES, by Giovanni Verga, translated and with an Introduction by D. H. Lawrence (1928).

THE STORY OF DR MANENTE. Being the tenth and last story from the suppers of A. F. Grazzini called *Il Lasca*. Translation and Introduction by D. H. Lawrence; Florence (1929).

Biography

THE INTELLIGENT HEART: The Story of D. H. Lawrence, by Harry T. Moore (1955)
—with some additional material this book is now reissued as *The Priest of Love*.

D. H. LAWRENCE: A Composite Biography. Gathered, arranged and edited by Edward Nehls; Madison (1957)
Vol. I: 1885–1919
Vol. II: 1919–1925
Vol. III: 1925–1930

D. H. LAWRENCE: The Man and his work: The Formative Years, 1885–1919, by Emile Delavenay (1972)
—translated, revised and abridged from the French, by K. M. Delavenay, originally published, 1969. A work of massive research, but not always reliable in its comprehension of Lawrence's language.

D. H. LAWRENCE: A Calendar of His Works, by Keith Sagar; Manchester (1979).

Some Memoirs and Critical Works

D. H. LAWRENCE: An American Interpretation, by Herbert J. Seligmann; New York (1924).

D. H. LAWRENCE, by F. R. Leavis; Cambridge (1930).

D. H. LAWRENCE, by Rebecca West (1930).

D. H. LAWRENCE: Two essays, by J. M. Murry; Cambridge (1930).

SON OF WOMAN: The Story of D. H. Lawrence, by J. M. Murry [1931].

YOUNG LORENZO: Early life of D. H. Lawrence, by Ada Lawrence and G. Stuart Gelder; Florence (1931).

THE SAVAGE PILGRIMAGE: A Narrative of D. H. Lawrence, by Catherine Carswell (1932).

D. H. LAWRENCE: An Unprofessional Study, by Anais Nin; Paris (1933)
—reissued, London 1961.

LAWRENCE AND BRETT: A Friendship, by Dorothy Brett (1933).

LAWRENCE AND 'APOCALYPSE', by Helen Corke (1933).

REMINISCENCES OF D. H. LAWRENCE, by J. M. Murry (1933).

D. H. LAWRENCE: Reminiscences and Correspondence, by Earl and Aschah Brewster (1934).

PILGRIM OF THE APOCALYPSE: A Critical Study of D. H. Lawrence, by Horace Gregory (1934).

NOT I, BUT THE WIND, by Frieda Lawrence; New York (1934)
—London edition, 1935.

D. H. LAWRENCE: A Personal Record, by E. T. [Jessie Chambers] (1935).

A POET AND TWO PAINTERS: A Memoir of D. H. Lawrence, by Knud Merrild (1938).

PORTRAIT OF A GENIUS, BUT . . . : The Life of D. H. Lawrence, 1885–1930, by Richard Aldington (1950).

D. H. LAWRENCE AND HUMAN EXISTENCE, by W. Tiverton (1951).

FIRE-BIRD: A Study of D. H. Lawrence, by Dallas Kenmare (1951).

D. H. LAWRENCE: Prophet of the Midlands, by V. de S. Pinto; Nottingham (1951).

JOURNEY WITH GENIUS: Recollections and reflections concerning the D. H. Lawrences, by Witter Bynner; New York (1953).

THE LOVE ETHIC OF D. H. LAWRENCE, by Mark Spilka; Bloomington (1955).

D. H. LAWRENCE: A Basic Study of His Ideas, by Mary Freeman; Gainesville, Florida (1955).

D. H. LAWRENCE: Novelist, by F. R. Leavis (1955).

THE DARK SUN: A Study of D. H. Lawrence, by Graham Hough (1956).

TRADITION AND D. H. LAWRENCE, by Richard L. Drain; Groningen (1960).

THE MEMOIRS AND CORRESPONDENCE, by Frieda Lawrence, ed. E. W. Tedlock (1961).

D. H. LAWRENCE, by Anthony Beal; Edinburgh (1961).

DARK NIGHT OF THE BODY: A Study of 'The Plumed Serpent', by L. D. Clarke; Texas (1964).

DOUBLE MEASURE: A Study of the Novels and Stories of D. H. Lawrence, by George H. Ford; New York (1965).

THE FORKED FLAME: A Study of D. H. Lawrence, by H. M. Daleski (1965).

THE ART OF D. H. LAWRENCE, by Keith Sagar; Cambridge (1966).

RIVER OF DISSOLUTION: D. H. Lawrence and English Romanticism, by Colin Clarke (1969).

D. H. LAWRENCE: The Critical Heritage, ed. R. P. Draper (1970).

THE VISUAL IMAGINATION OF D. H. LAWRENCE, by Keith Alldritt (1971).

D. H. LAWRENCE: A Critical Anthology, ed. H. Coombes; Harmondsworth (1973).

LAWRENCE, by Frank Kermode; London (1973).

THE PLAYS OF D. H. LAWRENCE, by Sylvia Sklar; London (1975).

THE LITERATURE OF FIDELITY, by Michael Black; London (1975).

THOUGHT, WORDS AND CREATIVITY: Art and thought in Lawrence, by F. R. Leavis (1976).

A D. H. LAWRENCE COMPANION, by F. B. Pinion; London (1978).

D. H. LAWRENCE: THE NOVELS, by Alastair Niven; Cambridge (1978).
LAWRENCE AND WOMEN, ed. Anne Smith; London (1978).
D. H. LAWRENCE, ed. A. H. Gomme; Sussex and New York (1978).

Note: Further information about Lawrence criticism can be had from Keith Sagar's *The Art of D. H. Lawrence* and from the checklist compiled by M. Beebe and A. Tommasi in *Modern Fiction Studies*, Vol. 5, No. 1, Spring 1959. For an account of the nature and chronology of Lawrence's literary development in the years 1913 to 1915, which differs in important ways from that put forward in the present essay, the reader is referred to 'The Marble and the Statue: the Exploratory Imagination of D. H. Lawrence', by M. Kinkead-Weekes, in *Imagined Worlds*, edited by M. Mack and I. Gregor, 1968.

Also mentioned in the text, *Autobiography*, Vol. II, 1914–44, by Bertrand Russell; London (1968).

WRITERS AND THEIR WORK

SHERIDAN: W. A. Darlington
SMART: Geoffrey Grigson
SMOLLETT: Laurence Brander
STEELE, ADDISON: A. R. Humphreys
STERNE: D. W. Jefferson
SWIFT: J. Middleton Murry (1955)
SWIFT: A. Norman Jeffares (1976)
VANBRUGH: Bernard Harris
HORACE WALPOLE: Hugh Honour

Nineteenth Century
ARNOLD: Kenneth Allott
AUSTEN: S. Townsend Warner (1951)
AUSTEN: B. C. Southam (1975)
BAGEHOT: N. St John-Stevas
THE BRONTË SISTERS:
                Phyllis Bentley (1950)
THE BRONTËS: I & II: Winifred Gérin
E. B. BROWNING: Alethea Hayter
ROBERT BROWNING: John Bryson
SAMUEL BUTLER: G. D. H. Cole
BYRON: I, II & III: Bernard Blackstone
CARLYLE: David Gascoyne (1952)
CARLYLE: Ian Campbell (1978)
CARROLL: Derek Hudson
CLOUGH: Isobel Armstrong
COLERIDGE: Kathleen Raine
CREEVEY & GREVILLE: J. Richardson
DE QUINCEY: Hugh Sykes Davies
DICKENS: K. J. Fielding
    EARLY NOVELS: T. Blount
    LATER NOVELS: B. Hardy
DISRAELI: Paul Bloomfield
GEORGE ELIOT: Lettice Cooper
FITZGERALD: Joanna Richardson
GASKELL: Miriam Allott
GISSING: A. C. Ward
HARDY: R. A. Scott-James
                and C. Day Lewis
HAZLITT: J. B. Priestley (1960)
HAZLITT: R. L. Brett (1977)
HOOD: Laurence Brander
HOPKINS: Geoffrey Grigson
T. H. HUXLEY: William Irvine
KEATS: Edmund Blunden (1950)
KEATS: Miriam Allott (1976)
LAMB: Edmund Blunden
LANDOR: G. Rostrevor Hamilton

LEAR: Joanna Richardson
MACAULAY: G. R. Potter (1959)
MACAULAY: Kenneth Young (1976)
MEREDITH: Phyllis Bartlett
MILL: Maurice Cranston
MORRIS: P. Henderson
NEWMAN: J. M. Cameron
PATER: Ian Fletcher
PEACOCK: J. I. M. Stewart
CHRISTINA ROSSETTI: G. Battiscombe
D. G. ROSSETTI: Oswald Doughty
RUSKIN: Peter Quennell
SCOTT: Ian Jack
SHELLEY: G. M. Matthews
SOUTHEY: Geoffrey Carnall
STEPHEN: Phyllis Grosskurth
STEVENSON: G. B. Stern
SWINBURNE: Ian Fletcher
TENNYSON: B. C. Southam
THACKERAY: Laurence Brander
FRANCIS THOMPSON: P. Butter
TROLLOPE: Hugh Sykes Davies
WILDE: John Stokes
WORDSWORTH: Helen Darbishire

Twentieth Century
ACHEBE: A. Ravenscroft
ARDEN: Glenda Leeming
AUDEN: Richard Hoggart
BECKETT: J-J. Mayoux
BELLOC: Renée Haynes
BENNETT: Frank Swinnerton (1950)
BENNETT: Kenneth Young (1975)
BETJEMAN: John Press
BLUNDEN: Alec M. Hardie
BOND: Simon Trussler
BRIDGES: J. Sparrow
BURGESS: Carol M. Dix
CAMPBELL: David Wright
CARY: Walter Allen
CHESTERTON: C. Hollis
CHURCHILL: John Connell
COLLINGWOOD: E. W. F. Tomlin
COMPTON-BURNETT: R. Glynn Grylls
CONRAD: Oliver Warner (1950)
CONRAD: C. B. Cox (1977)
DE LA MARE: Kenneth Hopkins
NORMAN DOUGLAS: Ian Greenlees

LAWRENCE DURRELL: G. S. Fraser
T. S. ELIOT: M. C. Bradbrook
T. S. ELIOT: The Making of
'The Waste Land': M. C. Bradbrook
FORD MADOX FORD: Kenneth Young
FORSTER: Rex Warner (1950)
FORSTER: Philip Gardner
FRY: Derek Stanford
GALSWORTHY: R. H. Mottram
GOLDING: Stephen Medcalf
GRAVES: M. Seymour-Smith
GRAHAM GREENE: Francis Wyndham
HARTLEY: Paul Bloomfield
A. E. HOUSMAN: Ian Scott-Kilvert
TED HUGHES: Keith Sagar
ALDOUS HUXLEY: Jocelyn Brooke
ISHERWOOD: Francis King
HENRY JAMES: Michael Swan
HANSFORD JOHNSON: Isabel Quigly
JOYCE: J. I. M. Stewart
KIPLING: Bonamy Dobrée
LARKIN: Alan Brownjohn
D. H. LAWRENCE:
                    Kenneth Young (1952)
D. H. LAWRENCE: I:
                    J. C. F. Littlewood (1976)
F. R. LEAVIS: Edward Greenwood
LESSING: Michael Thorpe
C. DAY LEWIS: Clifford Dyment
WYNDHAM LEWIS: E. W. F. Tomlin
MACDIARMID: Edwin Morgan
MACKENZIE: Kenneth Young
MACNEICE: John Press
MANSFIELD: Ian Gordon
MASEFIELD: L. A. G. Strong
MAUGHAM: J. Brophy
GEORGE MOORE: A. Norman Jeffares

MURDOCH: A. S. Byatt
NAIPAUL: Michael Thorpe
NARAYAN: William Walsh
NEWBY: G. S. Fraser
O'CASEY: W. A. Armstrong
ORWELL: Tom Hopkinson
OSBORNE: Simon Trussler
OWEN: Dominic Hibberd
PINTER: John Russell Taylor
POETS OF THE 1939-45 WAR:
                    R. N. Currey
POWELL: Bernard Bergonzi
POWYS BROTHERS: R. C. Churchill
PRIESTLEY: Ivor Brown (1957)
PRIESTLEY: Kenneth Young (1977)
PROSE WRITERS OF WORLD WAR I:
                    M. S. Greicus
HERBERT READ: Francis Berry
SHAFFER: John Russell Taylor
SHAW: A. C. Ward
EDITH SITWELL: John Lehmann
SNOW: William Cooper
SPARK: Patricia Stubbs
STOPPARD: C. W. E. Bigsby
STOREY: John Russell Taylor
SYNGE & LADY GREGORY: E. Coxhead
DYLAN THOMAS: G. S. Fraser
G. M. TREVELYAN: J. H. Plumb
WAR POETS: 1914-18: E. Blunden
EVELYN WAUGH: Christopher Hollis
WELLS: Kenneth Young
WESKER: Glenda Leeming
PATRICK WHITE: R. F. Brissenden
ANGUS WILSON: K. W. Gransden
VIRGINIA WOOLF: B. Blackstone
YEATS: G. S. Fraser